*THE SEXUAL
LIFE OF
CATHERINE M.*

THE SEXUAL

LIFE OF

CATHERINE M.

Catherine Millet

TRANSLATED FROM THE FRENCH

BY ADRIANA HUNTER

Grove Press / New York

Originally published in French as
La Vie Sexuelle de Catherine M. by Éditions du Seuil, Paris.

Published simultaneously in Canada
Printed in the United States of America

FIRST EDITION

Library of Congress Cataloging-in-Publication Data
Millet, Catherine.
[Vie sexuelle de Catherine M. English]
The sexual life of Catherine M. / Catherine Millet ; translated
from the French by Adriana Hunter.
p. cm.
ISBN 0-8021-1716-3
1. Erotic literature.   2. Women—Sexual behavior.   3. Sex.
4. Group Sex.   I. Title.
HQ463 .M4413 2002
306.7'082—dc21   2002020032

Grove Press
841 Broadway
New York, NY 10003

02 03 04 05   10 9 8 7 6 5 4 3 2 1

Contents

*THE SEXUAL
LIFE OF
CATHERINE M.*

1. Numbers

As a child I thought about numbers a great deal. The memories we have of solitary thoughts and actions from the first few years of life are very clear-cut: they provide the first opportunities for self-awareness, whereas events shared with other people can never be isolated from the feelings (of admiration, fear, love or loathing) that those others inspire in us, feelings that, as children, we are far less able to identify or even understand. I, therefore, have particularly vivid memories of the thoughts that steered me into scrupulous counting exercises every evening before I went to sleep. Shortly after my brother was born (when I was three and a half), my family moved into a new apartment. For the first few years we lived there, my bed was in the largest room, facing the door. I would lie staring at the light that came across the corridor from the kitchen where my mother and grandmother were still busying themselves, and I could never get to sleep until I had visualized these numerical problems one after the other. One of the problems related to the question of having several husbands. Not the possibility of the situation, which seems to have been accepted, but the circumstances themselves. Could a woman have several husbands at the same time, or only one after the other? In the latter case, how long did she have to stay married to each one before she could move on? What would be an "acceptable" number of husbands: a few, say five or six, or many more than that—countless husbands? How would I go about it when I grew up?

As the years went by, I substituted counting children for husbands. I imagine that, in finding myself under the seductive spell of some identified man (in turn, a film star, a cousin, etc.) and focusing my wandering thoughts on his features, I perhaps felt less uncertainty about the future. I could envisage in more concrete terms my life as a young married woman, and therefore the presence of children. More or less the same questions were raised again: was six the most "acceptable" number, or could you have more? What sort of age gap should there be between them? And then there was the ratio of girls to boys.

I cannot think back to these ideas without connecting them to other obsessions that preoccupied me at the same time. I had established a relationship with God that meant I had to think every evening about what he was going to eat, so the enumeration of the various dishes and glasses of water I offered him mentally—fussing over the size of the helpings, the rate at which they were served, etc.—alternated with the interrogations into the extent to which my future life would be filled with husbands and children. I was very religious, and it could well be that my confused perception of the identities of God and his son favored my inclination to counting. God was the thundering voice that brought men back into line without revealing him to them. But I had been taught that he was simultaneously the naked pink baby made of plaster that I put into the Christmas manger every year, the suffering man nailed to the crucifix before which we prayed—even though both of these were actually his son—as well as a sort of ghost called the Holy Spirit. Of course, I knew perfectly well that Joseph was Mary's husband, and that Jesus, even though he was both God and the son of God, called him "Father." The Virgin was in fact the mother of the Christ child, but there were times when she was referred to as his daughter.

When I was old enough to go to Sunday school, I asked to speak to the priest one day. The problem I laid before him was this: I wanted to become a nun, to be a "bride of Christ," and to become a missionary in an Africa seething with destitute peoples, but I also wanted to have husbands and children. The priest was a laconic man, and he cut short the conversation, believing that my concerns were premature.

Until the idea of this book came to me, I had never really thought about my sexuality very much. I did, however, realize that I had had multiple partners early on, which is unusual, especially for girls, or it certainly was among the milieu in which I was brought up. I lost my virginity when I was eighteen—which is not especially early—but I also had group sex a few weeks after my deflowering. On that occasion I was not the initiator, but I was the one who precipitated it—something I still cannot explain to myself. I have always thought that I just happened to meet men who liked to make love in groups or liked to watch their partners making love with other men, and the only reaction I had (being naturally open to new experiences and seeing no moral obstacle) was to adapt willingly to their ways. But I have never drawn any theory from this, and therefore have never been militant about it.

There were five of us, three boys and two girls, and we were finishing our lunch in a garden on a hill above Lyon. I had come to see a young man I'd met recently while staying in London, and I had taken advantage of the fact that a friend's boyfriend, André (from Lyon himself), was driving down from Paris. When I asked if we could stop on the way for me to pee quickly, André came and watched and stroked me as I squatted. It was not an unpleasant situation, but it did make me feel slightly ashamed, and it was perhaps at that precise moment that I learned to sidestep my embarrassment by burying my head between his legs and taking his cock in my mouth. When we reached Lyon, I stayed with André and we went to stay with a friend of his, a boy called Ringo who lived with an older woman whose house it was. The latter was away, and the boys had made the most of this and organized a little party. Another boy came and brought a girl, a tall, lanky, tomboyish girl with very short, coarse hair.

It was in June or July, it was hot and somebody suggested that we should all take our clothes off and jump into the big pond. I heard André's voice saying his girlfriend wouldn't be long joining in, and his words sounded a little muffled because I already had my T-shirt over my head. I forget when and why I stopped wearing underwear (even though as soon as I was thirteen or fourteen, my mother had made me wear an underwire bra and a panty girdle on the pretext that a woman "should be held in place"). In any event, I was naked almost immediately. The other girl started getting undressed, too, but in the end no one went in the water. The garden was exposed, and that is probably why the next set of images that come back to me are in a bedroom, me nestled in a tall cast-iron bed; all I can see through the metal bars are the brightly lit walls; I am aware of the other girl lying on a divan in one corner of the room. André fucked me first, quite slowly and calmly, which was his way. Then he stopped abruptly. I was overcome with an ineffable feeling of anxiety, just long enough to see him moving away, walking unhurriedly, his back arched, toward the other girl. Ringo came and took his place on top of me, while the third boy, who was more re-served than the other two, rested on one elbow beside us and ran his hand over my upper body. Ringo's body was very different from André's, and I liked it better. He was taller, more wiry, and one of those men who isolate the action of the pelvis from the rest of the body, who thrust without smothering, supporting their torso with their arms. But André seemed more mature to me (he was in fact older and had fought in the war in Algeria), his flesh was not so spare, he already had less hair, and I liked going to sleep cuddled up next to him with my buttocks against his belly, telling him we were a perfect fit. Ringo withdrew, and the one who had been watching and stroking me took his turn even though I had been resisting a terrible urge to urinate for some time. I had to go. The shy boy was piqued. When I came back, he was with the other girl. I no longer remember whether it was André or Ringo who took the precaution of telling me that he himself had only gone to "finish off" with her.

I stayed in Lyon for about two weeks. My friends worked during the day, and I spent my afternoons with the student I had met in London. When his parents were out, I would lie down on his cabin bed and he would lie on top of me, and I had to be careful not to knock my head against his shelves. I was still inexperienced, but I regarded him as even more of a novice than myself from the way he furtively slid his still slightly limp cock into my vagina, and the way he so quickly slumped his face down onto my neck. He must have been sufficiently preoccupied with what a woman's reaction might and should be to ask whether the sperm projecting onto the walls of the vagina produced a specific sensation of pleasure. I didn't know what to say. I didn't even feel his penetration that distinctly, much less to distinguish a viscous little puddle somewhere inside me. "Really, that's strange, no special feeling?" "No, nothing at all." He worried more than I did.

...

The little gang would come and wait for me late in the afternoon at the end of the road. They were happy and playful, and spotting them one day, the student's father said with a cordial note in his voice that I must be a hell of girl to have all these boys at my disposal. In fact, I had given up counting. I had completely forgotten my childhood investigation into the permitted number of husbands. I was not a "collector," and I thought that the boys and girls I saw at parties— mauling and being mauled and kissing until their breath gave out with as many people as possible so that they could boast about it the next day—were somehow offensive. I was happy simply to discover that the delicious giddiness I felt at the ineffably soft touch of a stranger's lips, or a hand fitting itself over my pubis, could be experienced an indefinite number of times because the world was full of men predisposed to do just that. Nothing else really mattered. I had nearly lost my virginity to a boy who made quite an impression on me. He had a slightly drooping face, huge lips and very black hair. My attraction was probably because no arm or hand had ever covered so much of my body as when I lay trapped by the sweater he had pulled up over my head, and my panties that he held taut against my groin. That was the first time I had felt myself in the grip of my pleasure. The boy asked me if I wanted more. I had no idea what that might mean, because I couldn't see what "more" I could possibly have. I brought the session to an end, and even though I continued this flirtation, meeting up with him regularly over the holidays, I never thought to take it further.

Neither was I particularly taken with the idea of going out with someone, or with several people. I fell in love twice, and with both men, any physical relationship immediately became impossible: the first man had just gotten married and, anyway, showed no interest in me at all; the second lived a long way away. I therefore had little desire to hook up with a boyfriend. The student was too bland, André was as good as engaged to my friend and Ringo had a long-term partner. In Paris there was my first lover, Claude, and he seemed to be in love with a bourgeois girl who would utter such poetic sentences as "Touch my breasts, they're so soft this evening" without letting him go any further. This example had quickly, if rather confusingly, taught me that I could not be classed as a great seductress, and that my place in the world was therefore not so much among the women facing the men, but alongside the men.

Put simply, there was nothing to stop me from constantly renewing the experience of tasting a different saliva every time and blindly feeling with my hand for a form that would always be unexpected, a surprise. Claude had a beautiful dick, it was straight and well proportioned, and the memory I have of those very first couplings is a feeling of fullness, heaviness, as if all of me had been stiffened and filled. When André opened his fly in front of my face, I was amazed to find something smaller and more malleable, because, unlike Claude, he was not circumcised. A dick that is constantly exposed demands to be looked at, it provokes sexual excitement with its smooth monolithic contours, whereas the foreskin that you can play back and forth, uncovering the glans like a great bubble forming on the surface of soapy water, elicits a more subtle sensuality, its suppleness spreading in waves to your own orifice. Ringo's dick was more like Claude's, the shy boy's more like André's, the student's belonged to a category that I would recognize later: those that, although not necessarily larger, are covered in a thicker outer layer, making them feel immediately more substantial in the hand. I discovered that every kind of dick required different movement, different behavior from me. And just as I had to adapt every time to another kind of skin, another complexion, different degrees of hairiness, different amounts of muscle tone (it goes without saying, for example, that not only do you hold on to a torso in a different way if it is smooth as a stone, or filled out with the beginnings of a bosom, or obscuring your view with a thatch of hair, but also that these images do not have the same resonance in your imagination: as a result, in retrospect, I seem to have been more submissive with the clean-cut or slightly rugged bodies that I perceived as truly male, whereas I took more initiative with heavier bodies that I feminized, however big they may have been), by the same token, the constitution of each body seemed to induce its own stances: I have pleasant memories of a very wiry body with a slender shaft that exclusively rammed into my ass as I offered it up into the air, thrusting in a series of jerks and as if from a distance, practically without touching any other part of my body apart from my hips, held in his hands; conversely, I didn't like it—not that I ever tried to get away—when fatter men, whom I nevertheless found attractive, covered me too fully and, matching their behavior to their corpulence, tended to give smoochy kisses and to lick my face. In short, I entered my adult sexual life in the same way that, as a child, I went into the tunnel of a haunted-house ride, blindly and for the pleasure of being jostled about and grabbed as chance would have it. Or, you could say, swallowed up by it as a frog is by a snake.

A few days after I got back to Paris, André sent me a letter to warn me, tactfully, that we all had the clap. My mother was the one who opened the envelope. I was sent to the doctor and banned from going out. But from then on, my own sense of propriety, which had become extremely intransigent, no longer tolerated living with my parents now that they could imagine me in the act of making love. I ran away from home, they brought me back; eventually, I left for good to go and live with Claude. The clap had been my baptism; for many years after, I lived in mortal terror of that scissoring pain, even though it struck me as being nothing more than a distinguishing sign, the shared fate of those who fuck a lot.

"Like a Nut"

In the biggest orgies in which I participated, from that time on, there could be up to about 150 people (they did not all fuck, some had come to watch), and I would take on the cocks of around a quarter or a fifth of them in all the available ways: in my hands, my mouth, my cunt and my ass. Sometimes I would exchanges kisses and caresses with women, but that was always less important. In the clubs, the proportion was far more variable, depending, obviously, on the clientele but also on the customs of each place—I will come back to that. It would be much more difficult to estimate the evenings spent in the Bois de Boulogne: should I count only the men that I sucked off with my head squashed next to their steering wheels, or those with whom I took the time to undress in the cabs of their trucks, and ignore the relay of faceless bodies behind the car doors, one hand maniacally rubbing up and down their cocks in diverse stages of erection while the other hand dived into the open car window to energetically knead my breasts? Today I can account for forty-nine men whose sexual organs have penetrated mine and to whom I can attribute a name or, at least, in a few cases, an identity. But I cannot put a number on those that blur into anonymity. In the situations I am describing here, even if there were people I knew or recognized at an orgy, the confused succession of embraces and couplings was such that if I could distinguish individual bodies or their attributes, I could not always distinguish the people themselves. And when I refer to the attributes, I have to admit that I did not always have access to all of them; some exchanges are very ephemeral, and if

I recognized a woman by the softness of her lips, I would not necessarily recognize her touch, which could be fiercely energetic. Sometimes I would realize only after the fact that I had been fondling a transvestite. I abandoned myself to the hydra. Until, that is, Éric broke away from the group to prise me out of it, in his own words, "like a nut from its shell."

I met Éric when I was twenty-one, not before his existence had been "announced" to me; some mutual friends had frequently assured me that, given my predispositions, he was perfect for me. After the holiday in Lyon I had continued having group sex with Claude. With Éric the regime intensified, not only because he took me to places where I could, as I have just shown, make myself available to an incalculable number of hands and penises, but more particularly because the sessions were well organized. To my way of thinking, there has always been a clear difference between, on the one hand, the more or less improvised situations that lead a group of people to redistribute themselves among the beds and sofas after a dinner, or that induce an excited gang of friends to drive around the Porte Dauphine in their car until they make contact with other cars and all the passengers end up intermingling in a large apartment; and, on the other hand, the soirees curated by Éric and his friends. I preferred the inflexible sequence of the latter and their exclusive goal: there was no rush and no tension; there were no outside factors (alcohol, demonstrative behavior, etc.) to impede the flow of our bodies. Their comings and goings never strayed from their ant-like determination.

. . .

Victor's birthday parties impressed me the most. At the entrance to his property there were guards with dogs, talking into walkie-talkies, and I was intimidated by the crowds of people. Some women had dressed for the occasion in transparent blouses or dresses; I was envious of them, and as people arrived and met up, sipping their champagne, I stood to one side. I only really relaxed after I had removed my dress or my trousers. My true outfit was my nudity, which protected me.

I was amused by the architecture of the place because it was similar to the decor of a then very fashionable boutique on the boulevard Saint-Germain, called the "Gaminerie." It was, on a larger scale than the boutique, a cave, with its attendant cells fashioned in white stucco. This "grotto" was underground, and its sole source of light came from the bottom of a swimming pool on the floor above. Through a pane of glass that formed a sort of vast television screen, we could see the succession of bodies diving in from the upper floor. I am describing a place I never moved through a great deal. The scale of things changed around me, but my situation was not very different from what it had been the first time, with my friends in Lyon. Éric would settle me on a bed or a sofa in one of the alcoves, respecting some vague custom by taking the initiative to undress me and put me on display. He might start to rub me and to kiss me, but then would immediately hand me over to others. I would almost always stay on my back, perhaps because the other most common position, in which the woman actively straddles the man's pelvis, is less adapted to intervention from several participants and, anyway, implies a more personal relationship between the partners. On my back, I could be stroked by several men while one of them, rearing up to make room and to see what he was doing, would get going in my sex. I was tugged and nibbled in several places at once, one hand rubbing insistently around the available part of my pubis, another skimming broadly across my entire torso or choosing to stroke my nipples . . .

I took pleasure in this caressing more than in the penetrations, in particular when it was a penis trailed over the entire surface of my face or a glans that rubbed against my breasts. I liked to catch one in my mouth as it passed by, running my lips up and down it while another came and begged attention on the other side of my outstretched neck, before turning my head to take the newcomer. Or having one in my mouth and one in my hand. My body opened up more under the effects of this kind of stroking, which was relatively brief and could be renewed again and again, than in penetration itself. On that subject, what I remember most is the stiffness between my legs after being pinioned sometimes for four hours, especially as many men tend to keep the woman's thighs spread well apart, to make the most of the view and to penetrate more deeply. When I was left to rest, I would become aware that my vagina was engorged. It was a pleasure to feel its walls stiffened, heavy, slightly painful, in their own way bearing the imprint of all the members that had labored there.

The position of the active spider in the middle of her web suited me well. Once—and this was not at Victor's house but in a sauna at the place Clichy—I hardly left the depths of a big armchair the whole evening, even though there was a huge bed in the middle of the room. With my head on a level with the dicks that came in range, I could suck one while, with my hands on the armrests, I jerked off two more. My legs were lifted up very high, and one after another, those who had become sufficiently aroused followed through in my cunt.

I sweat very little, but sometimes I was drenched in my partners' sweat. There would also be threads of sperm that dried along the tops of my thighs, sometimes on my breasts or my face, even in my hair, and men who are into orgies really like shooting their load in a cunt that's already dripping with cum. From time to time, on the pretext of going to the toilet, I would manage to extricate myself from the group and go to wash. Victor's house had a bathroom with a bluish light that was clear enough without being violent. A mirror took up the entire wall above the bath, and the deep, hazy image it reflected softened the atmosphere still further. I saw my body in it and was amazed to see that it was smaller, slimmer, than it had felt a few moments earlier. In the bathroom, more gentle exchanges took place. There was always someone there to compliment me on my olive skin or on the savoir faire I demonstrated with my mouth—and I didn't respond in the same way as when, buried under bodies, I could hear, as if from a long way away, a conversation about myself, rather like a sleeping patient making out the doctors' and the interns' comments as they made their rounds of the beds.

A jet of water on my gaping, swollen pussy. But few were the times when a man who had also come there for a pause did not make the most of the moment that I squatted over the bidet to jiggle his softened but always willing dick against my lips. And quite often, scarcely freshened up, I would stand and, putting my hands on the sink, offer my vulva to increasingly firm pressure from an organ that eventually managed to deliver a few thrusts. One of my favorite delights is the pleasure given by a penis slipping between the labia like that and then asserting itself there, progressively separating them, before burying itself in what I have had plenty of time to establish as an eagerly accommodating space. ✔

I have never had to suffer any kind of clumsiness or brutality, and I have generally been lucky with the attentiveness of my partners. If I was tired or the position was becoming uncomfortable, I only had to let it be known, often using Éric as my intermediary because he was never far away, and I would be left to rest or to get up. In fact, the unforced kindness, amounting almost to indifference, that surrounded me at orgies perfectly suited me as I was then, young and awkward in my relationships with other people. The population in the Bois de Boulogne was more mixed—socially, too—and I think that there I probably sometimes came across men who were even more shy than I was. I saw little of their faces, but I would catch some of them looking at me with something approaching caution in their eyes, or even amazement. There were the regulars who knew the place well and would briefly take the initiative in organizing the goings-on, and there were the more furtive ones, and there were also those who watched without joining in. Even though the venue and the participants changed from time to time, and Éric made it his job to find new arrangements—with me always following a little apprehensively—what paradoxically gave me pleasure was identifying familiar feelings in unusual circumstances.

One particular episode was full of contrasts. I had found a space on a concrete bench with a really rough, grainy surface. A group had formed: I had the pelvises of three or four men around my head, wanting me to take them in my mouth, but I could also catch glimpses of the pale hands of the outer circle as they traced a rhythmic action on their dicks in the darkness, like coiled springs quivering to the touch. Behind them were a few more shadows looking on. Just as someone was beginning to lift up my clothes, we heard the crunching sound of a car crash. I was left alone. We were in one of those clumps of trees planted along the boulevard de l'Amiral-Bruix near the Porte Maillot. I waited a moment and then went and joined the group in the clearing between the hedges. An Austin Mini had run straight into one of the lampposts down the center of the avenue. Someone said there was a young woman inside. A crazed little dog was running up and down. The bulb inside the lamppost and the car headlights were still on, creating a strange blend of yellow and white light. We must have heard the sirens of the emergency vehicles quite soon, because I went back to the bench. As if the space inside the little copse had been elastic, the circle formed again and the actors picked up the scene where it had been interrupted. A few words were exchanged; the sight of the accident suddenly reinforced what had been a tacit link between us, and there I was back with my ephemeral little community, completely at one with its focused and very unusual activity.

I liked slipping into the rare snatches of conversation and the ordinary gestures and positions that, in the Bois, both tempered and highlighted the more extraordinary encounters. One evening when the Porte Dauphine was virtually deserted, our car headlights picked out two very tall black men standing on the edge of the pavement. They looked as if they were lost or waiting, in this desolate backwater, for an improbable bus. They took me and Éric to a place nearby, to a small attic room. The room and the bed were both narrow. They took me one after the other. While one was on top of me, the other sat on the corner of the bed and made no attempt to join in. He just watched. They made big, slow movements and had long cocks like I'd never seen before, not too thick and able to penetrate very far without my having to spread my legs too wide. They were like twins. Two gentle, unhurried couplings in a row. They touched me with a sort of precision, and in return I reveled in the vast skin surface that they presented to me. I really think that, that particular time, I took the time to feel each stroke of their patient thrusting. While I was getting dressed, they chatted to Éric about the Bois de Boulogne and about their work as cooks. As we left they thanked me with all the sincerity of polite hosts, and my memory of them is full of affection.

At Chez Aimé, relations between people were not so civil. Aimé was a very popular swingers club. People came from very far away, even from abroad, to stay there. Years after it had closed, I still marveled like an awestruck schoolgirl when Éric listed the famous people—the film stars, singers, sports personalities and businessmen—I might have met there without actually opening my eyes enough to recognize them. During the time we went there, a film that parodied some aspects of the sexual revolution came out. One scene took place in a club that looked like Chez Aimé; it showed a group of men thronging round a table. There was a woman lying on the table, but all you could see were her legs, in high boots, jiggling comically over their heads. Because those sort of boots were in fashion at the time, and I wore them, and even tended to keep them on when I wasn't wearing a stitch of clothing because they were difficult to remove, and because I must have brandished them in the air like that more than once as I lay on a table, I was vain enough to think that it might well be my minimal attire and my waving in the air that had fired the director's imagination.

The pleasure that I felt as I succumbed to a long session at Chez Aimé with my buttocks parked on the edge of a big wooden table and the overhead light hanging down over my torso, as if I were some sort of board game, is equaled only by my loathing for the journey there. It was a long way from Paris: you had to drive through the sinister darkness of the Bois de Fausses-Reposes at Ville-d'Avray, and then you had to find the house at the bottom of a skimpy garden that looked like something from the suburbs of my childhood. Éric never gave me any warning of the evening's agenda because I think he drew some of his satisfaction from elaborating it with surprises; it was his own way of creating weird and wonderful situations. Anyway, I played along by asking no questions. Even so, when I gathered that we were heading there, I would worry not only at the thought of all the strangers who would soon be forcing me to wake up to where I was, but also in anticipation of the energy I would have to expend. It was a feeling not unlike the one I get before giving a conference, when I know I will have to be completely focused on what I am saying, and at the mercy of my listeners. Both the men met in those situations and the audiences plunged in darkness are faceless, and, miraculously, between the anxiety of anticipation and the weariness at the end, you are perfectly unaware of your own exhaustion.

Visitors went in Chez Aimé through the bar—I don't remember ever being taken in there (even though the feel of my pussy against the moleskin of a bar stool with my flattened buttocks lending themselves to furtive fondling belongs to my very oldest fantasies). I'm not sure I even paid much attention to what was going on around me, to the few women perched by the bar whose buttocks and thatches passersby certainly did uncover and play with. My place was in one of the back rooms, lying—as I have said—on a table. The walls were bare, there was no seating, there was nothing in these rooms except for the rough-hewn tables and overhead lights. So I could stay there two or three hours. Always the same configuration: hands running over my body, me grabbing at cocks, turning my head from left to right to suck, while other cocks rammed into me, up toward my belly. Twenty could take turns in an evening. That position, the woman on her back with her pubis on a level with the man's as he stands squarely on the ground, is one of the most comfortable I know. The vulva is well opened, the man in just the right place to thrust horizontally and strike deeply without stopping. It makes for a vigorous and precise fuck. I was sometimes set upon so violently that I had to hold on to the ends of the table with both hands, and for a long time I bore the scar of a little gash above my coccyx, where my spine had rubbed against the rough wood.

In the end Aimé closed. We went one last time; the place was deserted and Aimé himself, his bulk hovering behind the bar, was quietly but furiously railing at his wife. He had been summoned by the police. He was angry with her because she had persuaded us not to come back later.

That evening we ended up at Les Glycines, my first visit to a place that had seemed enchanting. Claude, a friend called Henri, and I made up the most amicable trio. Henri lived in a tiny apartment on the rue de Chazel, facing the pale, rough-cast surface of a high garden wall that hid a large private house. Because it was on our way, Claude and I used to stop off with Henri on our way home from our Sunday visit to our parents. The three of us would fuck together, both boys inside me at once—one in my mouth and the other up my ass or my cunt—under the playful gaze of one of Martin Barré's loviest paintings: we called it Spaghetti and the artist himself had given it to Henri. Afterward we would look out of the window, watching the comings and goings at Les Glycines. Henri had heard that the club was used by film stars, and sometimes we would think we'd recognized someone. We were just kids, the best kind of gawpers, fascinated and amused by this secret activity that we didn't even try to imagine, and actually more excited by the sight of things that were completely inaccessible to us: the swanky cars dropping people off, the classy deportment of the silhouettes who stepped out of them. When I went through the porch a few years later, I knew instantly that I preferred Chez Aimé's less spare style.

We went up a little gravel path blocked by a group of Japanese visitors who had been refused entry by the flight-attendantish girl at the door. The latter asked to see my Social Security card, to prove I was not a prostitute. Not being regularly employed, of course, I didn't have one, either on me nor

anywhere else. Even on the occasions when I was able to produce a pay stub, I would still be in the wrong because, even
today, whenever confronted by a woman taller than me, I turn
into an awkward child. We went in anyway. It was lit up like
a dining room, there were a lot of people lying naked on
mattresses on the floor, and what unsettled me even more than
the threat of the "employment officer" was that people were
telling jokes. A woman with very pale skin, no makeup and
tousled hair that still had the vestiges of the same French braid
as the hostess, was making everyone roar with laughter because her little boy "really wanted to come with her this
evening." I could see Éric, who was always very practical,
working his way along the baseboard looking for the outlet,
because we had managed to arrange a swap with a couple and
it would have been nicer to unplug the light. There were little
waitresses navigating amid the bodies, holding aloft trays of
champagne in flutes; one of them caught her foot in the elec-
tric cable and switched the light back on. She even accompanied the act with a loud "Shit." After that, I don't recall us
waiting for me to extract even the scantiest bodily emission.

Apart from in the Bois—even there, as we've seen, even
there!—you don't mix with people until you have greeted
them first, until you have respected a transitional moment in
which a few words are exchanged, where each person maintains just the time and space between themselves and the
others to offer a glass or hand over an ashtray. I always wanted
to abolish this suspense, but there were some rituals that I
tolerated better than others. Armand used to make me laugh
when, while everyone else was still at the chatting stage, he
would strip completely naked, incongruous by a few minutes

of anticipation, and fold his clothes as carefully as a butler. Or I would comply with what I thought was the stupid policy of one group who would not swing until they had eaten dinner, always in the same restaurant, like an old-school reunion; and what made their evening was to strip off the panties or stockings of one of the women in their party while the waiter was going around the table. On the other hand, I thought it was obscene to tell salacious stories at an orgy. Was it because I instinctively made a distinction between the playlets presented as a prelude to a play—the better to prepare you for it—and the playacting that serves only to delay it? The acts performed in the one are never performed in the other, where they really would be "out of place."

...

Even if I have kept some of the reflexes of a practicing Catholic to this day (secretly making the sign of the cross if I'm afraid something is going to happen, feeling watched as soon as I know I have done something wrong or made a mistake), I can no longer really pretend that I believe in God. It's highly possible that I lost this belief when I started having sexual relationships. Finding myself vacant, then, with no other mission to fulfill, I grew into a rather passive woman, having no goal other than those that other people set for me. I am more than dependable in my pursuit of these aims; if life went on forever, I would pursue them for all eternity, given that I did not define them myself. It is in this spirit that I have never wavered in the job I was given (a long time ago now), publishing *Art Press*. I was involved in its creation, and I have dedicated myself sufficiently to the work that I have become to some extent identified with it, but I feel more like a driver who must stick to the rails than a guide who knows where the port is. I've fucked in the same way. As I was completely available, I sought no more ideals in love than I did in my professional life; I was seen as someone with no taboos, someone exceptionally uninhibited, and I had no reason not to fill this role. My memories of orgies, of evenings spent at the Bois or with one of my lover-friends, are interlinked like the rooms in a Japanese palace. You think you are in a closed room until one of the partitions slides back, revealing a succession of other rooms, and if you step forward, more partitions open and close, and if the rooms themselves are numerous, the ways of passing from one to the other are infinite.

But trips to swingers' clubs hold little place in these memories. Chez Aimé was a different story: it was the very birthplace of fucking. And I have remembered the disappointment of Les Glycines because it was the exemplary realization of a dream I had carried with me since adolescence. Perhaps it is since my memory is chiefly visual that I remember more, for example, of Cleopatra—a club opened by some former customers of Chez Aimé, in an extravagant setting in the middle of a shopping center in the 13th arrondissement—than Les Glycines's neat decor and the activities to which I abandoned myself there; when all is said and done, they were quite banal. On the other hand, other places and other events are so vivid that I could almost file them by theme.

There would be the image of a lively line of cars, led by our own car. And as we are going up the service road on the avenue Foch, I have an urgent need to pee. Four or five cars slam on their brakes behind us. As I get out and run over the strip of grass to squat next to a tree, car doors start to open; a few people, misunderstanding my maneuver, come toward me. Éric rushes over to intercede, the place is open and very well lit. I get back into the car and the cortege sets off again. The parking lot at the Porte de Saint-Cloud: suddenly the attendant sees fifteen or so cars diving into the tunnel one after the other, then surfacing again, in exactly the same order, an hour later. During that hour, I was taken by about thirty men, several of them first held me up against a wall, and then they lay me on the hood. Sometimes the script is complicated by the fact that we have to shake off a few cars on the way. The drivers agree on a destination, a line of cars forms and is spotted by others who join it, but then the line is too long and it is wiser to limit the number of participants. One night we drove around for such a long time that it felt like the beginning of a journey. One driver knew of a place, and then he admitted that he was no longer sure of the way. Through the rear window I could see the pairs of headlights behind us navigating left and right, disappearing and reappearing. There were several stops, and several discussions, and eventually—in the bleachers of a sports stadium somewhere in Vélizy-Villacoublay—I had the pleasure of the patient pricks of those who had not gotten lost along the way.

Drifting could have been another theme. Cars trundle along, stop, set off again, brake abruptly like remote-control toys. Little ploy at the Porte Dauphine: we eye one another up from one car to the next, and the password seems to be "Do you have a place?" So some cars leave the circle, and we start on a sort of chase to an unknown address. Once, and it's true it was only once, the search went on a bit too long and we ended up doing something foolish. I am with a group of friends who don't know the Bois very well; there are six of us squashed into a Renault, and we're getting ready to go home after driving around in circles. We spot two or three cars down one of the many roads, we park alongside them and I, the brave and boastful little soldier going ahead in the name of all the others waiting behind me, go and give a blow job to the driver of the car behind us. As luck would have it, two policemen come and take up positions in front of me when I withdraw. They ask the man, who is awkwardly buttoning up, whether he paid me, and they take down everybody's name and address.

Even when a memory centers on physical facts, it is less the sensations than the atmosphere to be evoked first. I could gather together a good many anecdotes concerning the use to which, for years, I put my anus and, as frequently, if not more so, my vagina. In a beautiful apartment behind the Invalides, during a small-scale orgy, in a room on a mezzanine floor with a long bay window and floor-level lighting like you find on American film sets, I am taken in that orifice by the tool of a giant. Is it because the coffee table in the sitting room is a giant resin model of an open hand in which a woman could stretch herself out luxuriously that the place itself somehow feels disproportionate and unreal? I'm frightened of this great Cheshire cat's organ when I understand the route by which he is planning to penetrate, but he manages it without forcing too much, and I am amazed, and almost proud, that size represents no obstacle. Neither does number. Was it because I was ovulating or had a touch of the clap that at another orgy, a much larger one this time, I chose to fuck only with my ass? I can see myself at the foot of a very narrow staircase, in the rue Quincampoix, hesitating before deciding to go up. Claude and I were given the address by chance. We didn't know anyone. The apartment was very dark with a low ceiling. I could hear men nearby putting the word about, whispering, "She wants it up the ass," or warning someone who's heading the wrong way, "No, she only takes it from behind." That particular time it did hurt at the end. But I also had the personal satisfaction of having had no feelings of restraint.

Imaginings

As I read through the previous pages, still older images have come back to me, and these images were fabricated. How I conceived them, way before having my first experience and a very long time before I shed my innocence, constitutes a seductively appealing mystery. What shreds of the real world— photographs in Cinémonde; veiled comments of my mother's, like the time we left a café in which there was a group of young people, only one of whom was a girl, and my mother muttered that the girl must be sleeping with everyone; or the fact that my father came home late at night, funnily enough having just come from that café—did I pick up and thread together, and what instinctual material did I formulate so that the stories I told myself as I rubbed the lips of my vulva together so accurately prefigured my future sexual adventures?

I even remember a criminal case: the arrest of a rather obscure, aging woman (she must have been something like a maid on a farm) who was accused of killing her lover. I have forgotten the details of the murder because what really struck me was that among her belongings, they found notebooks that she had filled with memories and into which she pasted little relics—photographs, letters, locks of hair—connected with her lovers, who turned out to have been extraordinarily numerous. As a child I loved sticking bits of plants and flowers into my holiday project book, and I had a tidy scrapbook with precious photographs of Anthony Perkins or Brigitte Bardot, so I admired the fact that the woman had managed to collate this treasure, these traces of the men she had known, within a few simple notepads, and a secret corner of my libido was even more disturbed by the fact that this woman was ugly, and ended up alone, wild and outcast.

There are major structural similarities between situations I have lived and those I have imagined, even though I have never actively chosen to reproduce the latter in my life, and the details of what I have lived have had little part in nourishing my imaginings. Perhaps I should just assume that the fantasies forged in my earliest youth predisposed me to widely diverse experiences. Since I never felt ashamed of these fantasies, and I reworked and embellished them rather than trying to bury them, they offered not opposition to what was real but rather a sort of mesh through which real-life situations that other people might have found outrageous struck me as quite normal.

...

My brother and I were rarely taken to play in the park, but there was a little one that we crossed on the way to school. Down one side of the square there was a long wall with three pretty lean-tos along it. They were made of brick and wood, painted green and surrounded by shrubs. One was used for gardening tools, the other two housed the public toilets. There must have been groups of boys hanging about in the square. In any event, the very first narrative that accompanied my masturbating—and one that I used again and again for many years—put me in a situation where I was dragged into one of these shelters by a boy. I saw him kissing me on the mouth and touching me all over as his friends came to join us and they all started fondling me. We always remained standing, and I revolved in the middle of the tightly knit group.

Most Sunday mornings our parents would alternate on taking us to the matinee performance at the local cinema, whatever they were showing, and fleeting, barely-understood sequences glimpsed in romantic films and trailers; fired my imagination. I fantasized that I was allowed to go to the cinema alone. There were lots of people lining up. Suddenly someone would squeeze my ass. And again everyone else around me in the line would follow suit, and when I reached the ticket desk, the salesgirl could see that my skirt had been lifted up, and I would talk to her while someone rubbed themselves against my buttocks; I wouldn't have any panties on. The excitement would rise. My top would be off by the time I had crossed the foyer (I formulated an image of myself as an adult blessed with substantial breasts, an image I still resort to in my fantasies, whereas my breasts are actually average size). Sometimes the manager of the theater would ask us, calmly but with some authority, to wait until we were in the auditorium to get on with our disheveled embraces. At first I would wriggle about with one boy, squeezed up to him in the same seat. He was the rather taciturn gang leader who, having heated me to fever pitch, would then turn away abruptly and kiss another girl, abandoning me to his "men," and we would drop in a heap to the carpeted floor between the rows of seats. The narrative continues: perfectly respectable men could leave their seats and their suspicious wives to cross the auditorium in the dark and prostrate themselves on top of me. Sometimes I would have the lights turn back on during all this cavorting; or I would go to the bathroom and have a succession of comings and goings between there and the auditorium. I think sometimes I would have the police intervening. Another take: the manager would ask me to come to his office, then would call for all the boys, too. Another version: I would follow the group who had adopted me in the line all the way to a stretch of wasteland. And there, behind a picket fence, they would strip me naked and paw me. It was a compact group forming a circle around me, like a second fence screening me from view. One by one, the boys broke away from the circle to press themselves against me. In another version, I was nestled deep in a seat in a nightclub with a man on either side of me. While I busied myself with one of them and we kissed each other hungrily, the other stroked my body. Then I would turn around and kiss the second one, but the first would not let me go, or he would give up his place to a third man and so on; I kept swinging from left to right. I'm not sure that when I first started succumbing to these fantasies, I had ever done any petting or even kissed a single boy on the mouth. I was a late starter. When I came out of school, I would quite often meet up with a group of friends in the bedroom that I shared with my brother, but it was usually to have fights with them. At that sort of age, girls' bodies are more mature than boys'; I was quite well built and I would sometimes win.

...

If I am going back as far as my fantasy life during my childhood and adolescence, I should point out the initial disparity between fantasy and my actual behavior, especially, as I recall, at puberty. I had started reading a Hemingway novel (*The Sun Also Rises*, perhaps), and I was sufficiently disturbed by the description of one of the female characters, who was attributed several lovers, to stop reading the book. And I never went back to it. A conversation with my mother also gave me a shock. I don't remember how we got on to the subject, I can just see her setting the table in the kitchen as she confided in me that she had had seven lovers in her life. "Seven," she said, looking at me, "it's not all that many," but there was a shy questioning in her eyes. I scowled. It was the first time I had heard anyone say out loud that a woman could know more than one man. She became a bit defensive. A long time later, when I looked back on that rare moment of intimacy, I regretted my attitude. What was seven compared to a score that was still open?

When I was better informed about what sexual acts might entail, I integrated them into my imaginings, but coitus achieved did not preclude passing from one partner to another. One of the most detailed scenarios that illustrates this point of view was the following: I am the guest of a vulgar, fat man—pretending to be an uncle—at a business meal in a private salon in a restaurant. There are twenty or thirty men sitting down to eat, and my first contribution is to do the rounds, sucking each of them off under the table. I can picture their faces above me, surrendering saggily, as each of them successively, and briefly, lays out of the conversation. Then I get up onto the table and they amuse themselves finding interesting substitutes for me to take, cigars, sausages; someone eats a sausage from between my thighs. As the meal goes on, I am conscientiously fucked, some leading me off to a sofa, others taking me standing up, from behind, bent over the table, while the discussions go on around us. The maître d' and the waiters have their turns. If my masturbating has not yet been ended by an orgasm, then the kitchen boys finish me off. Finding myself in a group of men getting on with their different jobs, stopping only to join me in a casual, offhand way, is a recurring scenario. A subtle alteration turns the uncle into a stepfather, and the conference into men playing cards (or watching football), and they take turns fucking me on a sofa while the others get on with their hand (or gesticulate at the television screen).

All my life I have gone back over, tinkered with and developed these few imagined situations with the application of a musician composing a fugue, and those that serve me today are more or less altered versions of these originals. I mentioned brief film sequences that gave rise to certain fantasies. I saw only an extract of Éric Rohmer's *La Collectionneuse* when it came out, on television perhaps. In a vacation house, a man goes into a room and walks past a couple making love on the bed with perfect indifference; he just catches the young woman's eye. As I have gone back to this sequence again and again, my own transposition has created this: a deliveryman comes into my house, although—oddly—I don't have to open the door for him, and he finds me in my bedroom (where the half-light is very like that in the film), watching a pornographic video. Without a word, he lies down on top of me and is soon replaced by a second deliveryman, then a third, both of whom behave just as naturally. The story sometimes continues: a male friend is coming to pick me up, and I have to get ready. I carry on fucking while standing up, taking care not to smudge my makeup or rumple my clothes, with my skirt lifted up over my back. The friend then takes the trouble to ring the door-bell, and I go to let him in, waddling like a duck with one of the deliverymen's dicks burrowed in my cunt from astern. The friend, aroused himself, quickly undoes his fly, etc.

...

Sexual fantasies are far too personal for them to ever really be shared. Still, I had a powerful imagination, and this gave me a well I could draw from when, later, I started meeting talk-ers. In my experience, most men make do with a few expres-sions and catchphrases; you're their "little cocksucker," you're "a talented ball eater" before entering the ranks of the "little slut who's not too ashamed to go on like that all night," and you will rarely be "rammed right up to the hilt" or "fucked good and deep" without the incident being announced out loud. You encourage them, admitting that you're just a "bitch in heat," and as they reassure you that you're going to get "rammed," "nailed" or "plugged," you gasp and say "it's so big," "it's so hard" and "it's so good" until you eventually "swallow the spurt," like the cat that got the cream. But these are merely accentuations, reiterations punctuated by the mantra of interjections, gruntings and all the inflections of the usual cries. Because, paradoxically, these words need less reciprocation than caresses do, dirty words are always more stereotyped, and perhaps some of their power derives from the very fact that they belong to the most immutable inheritance. So, in the end, even words—which should help to distinguish us from each other—serve to fuse us all together and to accelerate the annihilation of the senses that we are all trying to achieve in those moments.

It is quite another story to construct a complete running commentary throughout the act, given by two voices, in counterpoint to the physical exchange.

Another man immeasurably—and quite fantastically—widened my understanding of fornicatory communion. He started the conversation by saying that he was going to take me to a hotel; there was little point in specifying what sort. There would be men lining up by the bed, all the way out to the corridor. How much did I think they would pay to shoot their load in my cunt? I suggested: "Fifty francs?" The correct sum was whispered quietly in my ear: "That's far too much. No, they'll give twenty francs to fuck you from the front and thirty to give it to you up the ass. How much of it are you going to take?"

Knowing that I always underestimate, I ask, "Twenty?" A hard thrust of his dick given as a warning shot: "Is that all—thirty!?" Another stab in my vagina: "You'll take a hundred and you won't wash."

"There'll be young boys who'll shoot their load almost before they get inside me."

"They'll do it on your stomach and your tits, too, you'll be covered in it."

"Yes, and there'll be some who are very old and very dirty, they won't have washed for so long that they'll have scabs on their skin."

"Yes, and how much would you take to let them piss on you?"

"Will some of them shit on me too?"

"Yes, and you'll lick their asses afterward."

"And will I refuse to at first? Will I fight?"

"Yes, and they'll smack you."

"It's disgusting, but I'll clean out the folds of their assholes with my tongue."

"We'll get there in the evening, and you'll stay there till the following morning."

"But I'll get tired."

"You will be able to sleep, they'll keep on fucking you. And we'll come back that evening, and the hotel manager will bring his dog, and there'll be someone who'll pay to see you doing it with the dog."

"Will I have to suck it?"

"You'll see, it'll have a very red cock and it'll climb on top like you're a bitch and stay stuck inside you."

Other times the events would unfold in the workmen's shed on a construction site, and whole teams of workmen would file through, paying no more than five francs a go. As

I have suggested, my body sometimes convulsed in response to these images, but not always; the real action and the fantasy scrolled in tandem and merged only sporadically. We spoke in measured tones with all the precision and attention to detail of two scrupulous witnesses helping each other reconstruct a past event. When he came close to orgasm, my partner became less talkative. I don't know whether he was concentrating on one of the images of our imaginary film. As for me, I would sometimes bring the scenario back to a more private situation. The shed on the building site would become the caretaker's quarters in a building undergoing repairs. In those sorts of cramped spaces, the bed is sometimes just hidden behind a curtain. Only my stomach and legs were visible in front of it, and the workmen still kept coming in droves to service me without my seeing them or their seeing me, under the gaze of the caretaker who regulated the traffic.

Communities

There are two ways of envisaging a multitude, either as a crowd in which individual identities become confused, or as a chain where, conversely, what distinguishes them from one another is also what binds them, as one ally compensates for another's weaknesses, as a son resembles his father even while he rebels. The very first men I knew immediately made me an emissary of a network in which I couldn't hope to know all the members, the unwitting link in a family of biblical scale and diversity.

I have already explained that I was reticent in social relationships and saw the sexual act as a refuge into which I willingly abandoned myself: it was a way to avoid looks that embarrassed me and conversations for which I was ill prepared. There was, therefore, no question of my taking any initiative. I never flirted or tried to score. On the other hand, I was completely available: at all times and in all places, without hesitation or regret, by every one of my bodily orifices and with a totally clear conscience. If, as Proust's theory goes, I see my own personality in terms of the image that other people have made of it, then that is the dominant trait. "You never said no, never refused anything. You didn't put on airs." "You were far from inert, but you weren't demonstrative, either." "You did things so naturally, you were neither reticent nor dirty, just a tad masochistic from time to time." "At an orgy, you were always the first to jump in, right out there in front." "I remember Robert would send a taxi for you as if there was some emergency, and you would go." "People thought of you as some sort of phenomenon; even with an incredible number of guys, you would still be the same, right up to the end, at their mercy. You weren't playing the little woman who wants to please her man, or the ball-buster. You were a friend who happened to be a girl, a girlfriend." And also this note that a friend put in his diary, which still gives me a glow of pride: "Catherine, who deserves the highest praise for her calmness and availability in every situation."

. . .

The first man I knew introduced me to the second. Claude was friendly with a couple, colleagues some ten years older than us. The man was not very tall, but he had the muscle tone of a sportsman; she had magnificent, slightly Asian features, with short-cropped blond hair; she also had one of those stiff personalities with which intelligent women sometimes modulate their sexual freedom. It could be that Claude had had some sexual encounters with her before introducing me to the man, before, that is, arranging for me to fuck him. We carried on a sort of loosely arranged partner swap that continued even after Claude and I had rented a studio next to their apartment. I would go and meet the man at their apartment, while the woman would join Claude in ours. The wall was like a television remote control: there was a different film on if you switched sides. There was only one occasion when this disjunction was not respected. It was while we were on holiday in a house that they owned in Brittany. A cold, mellow afternoon light permeated the sitting room, right into the corner where the man was resting on a daybed. I was sitting at the foot of the bed, the woman was in and out, Claude had gone off somewhere. The man gave me that weak, almost submissive look that some men have even when they are expressing the most imperious of orders, drew me to him, held my chin and kissed me, then pushed my head down toward his penis. I liked it better like that—using me to harden him up while I lay curled in on myself rather than stretching up to his face for a long kiss. And I sucked him off well. Perhaps it was on that day that I realized I had a gift for it. I concentrated on coordinating the way I moved my hand

and my lips; from the pressure of his hand on my head, I knew when I should speed up the rhythm or slow it down. But it was definitely the facial expressions that I remember most clearly. When I occasionally looked beyond the immediate horizon of his zipper to take a deep breath, I saw her expression—as gently vacuous as a statue—and his, almost disbelieving. I now feel it was then I first hazily grasped the fact that if relationships with friends could spread and grow like a climbing plant, twisting and knotting together in perfect and reciprocal freedom, and that all you had to do was to let yourself go with the flow of its sap, then this was all the more reason for me to decide on my own behavior for myself, resolutely and solitarily. I like this paradoxical solitude.

...

The art world is made up of a multitude of communities or families, and their rallying points—at the time when I started working as a critic—were more places of work, galleries and the editorial offices of magazines, than cafés. Naturally these little networks were breeding grounds for casual romances. As I lived right on Saint-Germain-des-Prés, which was where the modern-art galleries all were at the time, there was not far to go between an exhibition and a little cuddle. I can see myself on the pavement of the rue Bonaparte with a new painter friend, a shy boy who never really looked up as a smile spread across his face or as he peered at you through his thick glasses. I don't remember how he led me to understand that he wanted me, probably very warily ("I'd like to make love to you, you know"), perhaps even without touching me. Most likely I didn't give much of a reply. What I do remember was how resolute I was. I took him all the way to my room. He let himself be led without realizing that he was urging me on, too, weighing me down with those subjugated, tentative eyes. My pleasure derives from the precise moment when I have made the decision and the other feels a bit taken aback. I have an intoxicating feeling of fulfilling a heroine's destiny. But the best thing to put him at his ease is the girl-who's-just-escaped-her-parents'-clutches speech: I explain daffily that "I want everything." He carries on, encouraging me with his attentive eyes. Someone who once took the same route has since admitted that my room under the eaves reminded him of a place you might rent by the hour, and that the rather coarse fabric serving as a bedcover seemed like a tarpaulin to protect it from the activities that were about to take place.

A group visit to an exhibition organized by Germano Celant in a Genoa museum. Claude, Germano and the others are walking ahead; I spend a little longer in each gallery, accompanied by William, who has contributed to the exhibition. With quick, furtive gestures, he lands his hand across my snatch, I grind the bulge in his trousers, amazed to find it so hard, like an inanimate object, not like part of a living body. He has a very distinctive laugh, which sounds as if his mouth is already engaged in a long, deep kiss. He's having fun teaching me English: cock, pussy. Not long after that, he spends a few days in Paris. As he comes out of the Rhumerie, he licks my ear and whispers in English, "I want to make love with you," leaving a little pause between each of the words. In the corner next to a service door at the back of the post office that stands where the rue des Rennes meets the rue du Four,

I mutter my own English contribution: "I want your cock in my pussy." Explosive laughter, the same trip all the way to the studio on the rue Bonaparte. William, like Henri and like many others, would return several times. We fuck there as a twosome and with others. The pretext is often a girl picked up by one of the boys, who needs a bit of persuading that it's even greater fun when there are more than two to share in the pleasure. It doesn't always work, and when it doesn't, I am given the job of reassuring her, consoling her. The boys disappear discreetly to have a cigarette on the landing. I don't actually speak, I cajole, give her a gentle hug; girls are more easily convinced by another girl. Of course they could just leave, but not one of them ever did, not even the one who remained friends with Claude and admitted, twenty years later, that it was because she was still a virgin that she had refused to comply that evening and burst into tears. Henri remembers another girl: I locked myself into the kitchen—which also served as a bathroom—with her to clean her face because her tears had smudged her mascara. He maintains that from the communal toilets on the landing, he could hear us moaning through the skylights. She probably wanted to thumb her nose at the boys, and I, perversely, played along with her.

By a curious inversion of sensitivity, although I am relatively blind to a man's seductive maneuvers—quite simply because I prefer them to be kept to a minimum, but I will come to that subject shortly—I am always well aware when a woman is attracted to me, not that I have ever expected a woman to give me any pleasure. Oh, I am not denying the devastating delight of touching smooth, rounded, delicate skin, which most women's bodies offer and only a very few men's. But I have joined in these embraces and their related fumblings only so as not to break the rules of the game. In fact, men who always suggest this sort of threesome strike me as boring and unimaginative, and I quickly tire of them. I do, however, love looking at women myself. I could make out an inventory of the wardrobes, guess the contents of the makeup bags, even describe the physiques of the women I work with better than their own male partners could. Out in the streets, I follow them and watch them more tenderly than any man trying to pick them up; I associate a particular conformation of the buttocks with a certain style of panties, a particular wiggle in a walk with the height of a heel. But my excitement is limited to a visual satisfaction. Beyond that I feel just a communal sympathy for hardworking women, for the huge fraternity of women who have the same first name as me (one of the most common names in France after World War II) and for the valiant warriors of sexual liberation. As one of them once told me (and she herself was a genuine and affectionate dyke but also a swinger): "*Si être copains, c'est partager le pain, alors nous sommes de vraies copines*" [If being *copains* (male friends) means sharing bread (*le pain*), then we're truly *copines* (female friends) because we share dicks (*pines*)].

There was an exception at an improvised orgy where half the participants had brought along the other half, who were novices. I found myself alone for a long time on the thick black carpet of the bathroom with a blonde who had curves everywhere: her cheeks, her neck, her breasts and buttocks, of course, even down to her ankles. I was struck by her majestic name; she was called Léone. Léone had taken some persuading before going with the flow. Now she was completely naked, like a golden Buddha in his temple. I was a little lower, because she was sitting on the step that ran all the way around the raised bath. How had we ended up in that confined space when it was a huge, comfortable apartment? Perhaps because she had been indecisive and I, once again, had felt compelled to take on the role of attentive facilitator? My whole face burrowed noisily in her fleshy vulva. I had never sucked on such a swollen extremity, and it really did fill my mouth, as those from the South of France say, like a giant apricot. I latched on to her labia like a leech, then I dropped the fruit and stretched my tongue so far I almost tore its root, the better to dive into the extraordinary softness of her opening, a softness that makes the smoothness of breasts and shoulders pale into insignificance. She was not the wriggling sort, she let out short, little moans, as soft as everything else about her. They resonated with sincerity and gave me a tremendous feeling of exultation. I put myself to work suckling the small raised knot of flesh; it was so good to let myself go as I listened to her raptures! While we all got dressed again, amid the fun and confused atmosphere of a locker room, Paul, who spoke with less fact than the others, turned to her and asked: "So? That was good, wasn't it? Don't we think she was right to let herself be talked into it?" She lowered her eyes and put a lot of emphasis on the first word as she replied that one person had certainly made an impression on her. I thought: "Please, God, let it be me!"

...

We had found a ready-made philosophy by reading Bataille, but when Henri and I look back on that fevered period, I think he is right to say that our sexual obsession and our missionary zeal derived more from a youthful playfulness. The bed in that tiny apartment was positioned in an alcove, which reinforced the feeling of snuggling in a hiding place, and when four or five of us thrashed about on it together, it meant only that supper had turned into a round of "I'll show you mine if you'll show me yours": the diners had tickled one another's parts under the table with their bare feet, or perhaps someone had proudly raised up a finger covered in a clear and slightly redolent sauce. Henri would make a game of it by bringing along a girl he had met just half an hour earlier in some arcade, and it was an adventure for our whole team to wander the streets at four o'clock in the morning, looking for some poor girl's apartment, bent on disturbing her tidy bed. Half the time the ploy failed. The girl would let herself be fingered, would let someone take off her bra or her tights, but would end the evening clamped to a chair explaining that she really couldn't, but yes, she was very happy to watch, that was fine with her, yes, she would wait till someone could drive her home. I've sometimes caught glimpses of people, men or women in fact, taking refuge on an incongruous upright chair or balancing their buttocks on the edge of the sofa, unable to take their eyes off the pale limbs flailing in the air a few inches away, a few inches which put them in a whole different time zone. They don't take part, so you cannot really say that they are fascinated. Lagging behind—or shooting on ahead—they are the patient, studious viewers of an edifying documentary.

Our zeal was, of course, only skin-deep, because the challenges we set were intended far more for ourselves than for those we tried to initiate. Henri and I once failed on the boulevard Beaumarchais in one of the big, bourgeois apartments whose intellectual owners lived with bare parquet floors and inadequate overhead lighting. The friend who welcomes us has a thick beard, permanently parted by his bland laugh; he is married to a modern woman. All the same, she balks and goes to bed. We play at transgression, and I seem to remember quivering and roaring with laughter between their streams of urine. No, no, Henri corrects me, he was the only one to piss on me. In any event, what is certain is that we took the precaution of getting into the huge cast-iron bath. Then the three of us did go and fuck a bit on the balcony.

One of my girlfriends puts me up for some months. I sleep in a tiny, unfurnished attic room, sometimes with the cats for company. When her boyfriend comes to see her, she leaves the door to her bedroom wide open and neither of them makes any attempt to contain their exclamations. It never occurs to me to join them. I don't get involved in other people's business, and anyway, snuggled in my narrow bed, I think of myself almost as their little girl. But with that stubbornness peculiar to children and animals, I make quite sure that they get involved with my business. Given that, to some extent, I share her life, there is no reason why my beautiful hostess shouldn't systematically take the same cocks between her thighs as I do. It works four or five times. She resolutely allows herself to be pinned to the bed, her legs waving in the air like butterfly wings. I really like it when she looks right at Jacques (whose dick is reverberating from the twang of elastic when he pulled off his underwear) and says loudly that he's "hung like a horse." That was Jacques, who would become my husband, but with whom, at the time, I was just beginning to get together. He now reminds me that I once had a tantrum and set about kicking him wildly when he was fucking her. I had forgotten that, too. Although I remember how I myself would niggle at the jealousies that other people never admitted. I feel as if I'm in a film about the free and easy lives of the young bourgeoisie when I go early one morning—stopping at the boulangerie on the way—to wake Alexis, who lives in a cute duplex on the rue des Saints-Pères. I notice the coolness of my skin next to his warm pajamas, a bit moist as I like it. He likes making fun of my promiscuity, and he says that, at least at this time of day, he can be sure of being the first person of the day to penetrate me. Well, no, he isn't, actually! I spent the night with someone else, and we had a fuck before I left; his come is still in my pussy. I stifle my exuberant laughter in the pillow. I can tell that Alexis is a little upset.

Claude told me to read *The Story of O,* and there were three ways in which I identified with the heroine: I was always ready; my cunt certainly wasn't barred with a chain, but I was sodomized as often as I was taken from the front; and finally, I would have loved her reclusive life in a house isolated from the rest of the world. Instead, I was already very active in my professional life. But the convivial atmosphere of the art world, the facility with which—despite my fears—I formed connections with people, and the fact that these connections could so easily take a physical turn led me to believe that the space in which this sort of activity was carried out was a well-regulated, closed world. I have already used the word "family" several times. Sometimes this metaphor has not been a metaphor. For a long time I kept the adolescent trait of exerting my sexual attraction within a family circle, when a boy or a girl goes out with someone and drops him or her to go out with a brother or sister, or a cousin. I was once involved with two brothers along with their uncle. I was a friend of the uncle and he often brought along his two nephews, who were even younger than I. Unlike when this man would take me to meet friends of his, there was no pre-amble or stage management on these occasions. The uncle would get me going and the two brothers would nail me. I would relax afterward, listening to their men's talk, some new home-improvement gadget or computer software.

I am still on friendly terms with a number of men whom I first knew as regular sexual partners. In other cases, we have lost touch. I remember most of these acquaintances with genuine pleasure. When I worked with some of them, I found that the enduring intimacy and tenderness facilitated our collaboration. (Only once did I get angry about a serious work matter.) What's more, I never remove a person from his own network of friends and relationships or from the activities he enjoys. I had met Alexis as part of a group of young critics and journalists who were trying to set up new artistic pub-lications. I was fucking two other people on the same circuit, and in fact Alexis had asked me, rather tartly, whether I had set myself a schedule to be "fucked by every young critic in France." We worked in a "school's out" sort of atmosphere, and my two other colleague-lovers, unlike Alexis, were still a bit rough around the edges even though they were already married. They both had pimply faces and did not exactly take good care of themselves. I gave in to one of them because, having been lured to his apartment on the pretext of a translation that needed checking through (another one of those cramped little apartments on Saint-Germain-des-Prés), he had whined that, seeing I was sleeping with everyone, it would be really mean if I didn't sleep with him. The other had tried his luck more confidently. He had arranged to meet me at his publisher's office, and the receptionist told him I had arrived, adding—with the consideration typical of women in her profession—that the young woman waiting for him in reception was not wearing a bra under her blouse. The sexual relationship with the first man came to a pretty abrupt halt, but with the second it went on for several years. Later, they became collaborators on *Art Press* and stayed there a long time.

I have suggested that I met Éric through his friends, after hearing what they had to say about him. Among these friends was Robert, whom I met while putting together a piece on art foundries. In the event, he took me to a foundry in Le Creusot where he was having a monumental sculpture cast. We traveled back at night, and, during the trip Robert joined me in the back of the car and laid full-length on top of me. I didn't bat an eye. It was a narrow car, and I was sitting sideways in my seat with Robert's head resting on my abdomen, and my pelvis hanging over the edge to facilitate his groping. From time to time I would put my head down and he would give me little kisses. Glancing in the rearview mirror, the driver commented that I seemed out of it. In fact, the situation left me as dumbfounded as the visits to the foundries with their gigantic ovens. I saw Robert almost daily for quite a long time, and he introduced me to a lot of people. I could instinctively tell those with whom the relationship could take a sexual turn and those with whom it would not. An instinct that Robert also had: as a way of putting some of them off, he had come up with the idea of warning them that, as an art critic, I was beginning to wield some power.

It was Robert who told me about that myth of Parisian life, Madame Claude. I had long fantasized about being a high-class prostitute, although I was neither tall nor beautiful, which I had been told you needed to be, nor distinguished enough for the job. Robert used to joke about the combination of my sexual appetite and my professional curiosity; he would say that I could write a piece about plumbing if I went out with a plumber. And he always maintained that, given my personality, the person I had to meet was Éric. But in the end, I met the latter through a mutual friend of theirs, a very edgy boy, one of those types who pounds into you with mechanical power and regularity, and someone with whom I had spent some exhausting nights. In the morning, as if that wasn't enough, the friend would take me to the huge studio he shared with his work partner, and there, languidly tired, I would let this other man come over and take me in his silent, almost serious way. One evening the friend invited me to go and have dinner with him and Éric. As we already know, Éric introduced me to more men than anyone else, friends, colleagues and strangers. For the sake of full disclosure, I must add that, at the same time, he introduced me to a rigorous way of working to which I still adhere.

For obvious reasons, the pattern in which these relationships emerged, and the way in which individual incidents and deeds are recalled, overlap with aesthetic groupings. A painter friend called Gilbert, with whom I am reminiscing about my early beginnings, remembers that I restricted myself to discreet fellatio when I joined him in the afternoons in the apartment he shared with his family. Penetration was reserved for when he came to see me at my home. On the first of these visits, he didn't "finish" very satisfactorily; at the last minute I asked him to switch to my ass. Such was my primitive method of contraception, bolstered by the image I had of my body as an integrated whole with no form of hierarchy in terms of either morals or pleasure, and each of its individual parts could, insofar as was possible, be substituted for any other. It was actually another painter of the same school who made a point of teaching me to put my cunt to better use. I had shown up at his studio early one morning for an interview, not knowing I was going to find a very good-looking and forthcoming man. I don't think I left until the following day. As is often the case in artists' studios, the bed was positioned under a glass roof or a window, as if to establish what was going on within a framework of light. My eyelids can still feel the powerful light flooding onto my upturned head and blinding me. I must have had the same reflex of slipping his dick into my anus, just like that. Afterward, he talked to me. He told me extremely persuasively that one day I would meet a man who would know how to take me from the front and to bring me to orgasm that way, and that it would be better than the other. Gilbert can't believe it when I tell him that at the time I was seeing yet another of his painter friends (the near-sighted one whose insistent gaze carried me), who he thought had never cheated on his wife; on the other hand, Gilbert himself reminds me of a third man with whom

I used to participate in foursomes, still in the little studio on the rue Bonaparte, and who used to talk about the boys having sex between themselves. But I am convinced that this was probably just a fantasy.

When William became part of an artists' collective, I found myself spending the night with John, one of the members of the group. I had already met him several times, and we had even spoken at conferences together. I found him very attractive; he gave speeches about theory that my approximative understanding of English turned lurid, and as he talked, the movements of his lips accentuated his fine young cheekbones. I had come to New York to meet Sol LeWitt, who had just started doing his works in torn and crumpled paper. When I arrived, I rang William from the airport to ask him to put me up. I can see us now, standing in the loft he had recently moved into, devouring each other with kisses, and him encouraging John to do the same. The walls went only three quarters of the way up to the ceiling and were arranged at right angles to form rooms that seemed laid out in random cubes like a child's bricks. Four or five people came and went, apparently absorbed in some private task. William picked me up and carried me over to a mattress behind one of the walls. John was very gentle, providing a great contrast to William's nervous, abrupt movements. William left us, and eventually John went to sleep. We had curled up together with his hand clamped onto my pubis. Early the following morning I had to extricate myself from his viselike grip with the slow deliberate maneuvers of a contortionist, and to crawl out of the sheets onto the floor because, despite the light that was pouring in through the skylights, he was still asleep. I ran into the street, caught a taxi to the airport and barely caught my flight. Even though I continued to follow that group's work, I didn't see John again for many years. When I did, during a retrospective, we exchanged but a few words because I found it so difficult to understand what he was saying.

...

As time went by, my shyness in social situations was replaced by boredom. Even among friends whose company I enjoy, even if I follow the conversation at first and am no longer afraid to join in, there always comes a moment when I suddenly lose interest. It's a question of time: all of a sudden I have had enough; whatever subject we are tackling, I feel as if I'm turning to stone, like when I watch one of those TV soaps that recreates humdrum domesticity too accurately. It is irreversible. In these instances, tacit gestures—sometimes unseen ones—provide some escape. Even though I am not very enterprising, I have often improvised a little pressure from my thigh or a little crossing of ankles with the man next to me at the table, or—better still—the woman (it is less likely to have repercussions) in the hopes of feeling that I am really a distant observer of this earnest assembly, busying myself with something else somewhere else. In the context of communal life—on holiday, for example, when a group of people does all sorts of things together—I have often felt the need to absent myself from outings and meals by acting randomly when the need arose. There were some particularly frenetic summers, defined by the incessant traffic between sexual partners, sporadically united in small orgies under the sun behind the low wall of a garden that overlooked the sea, or at night in the comings and goings between the many bedrooms of a villa.

One evening I decide not to join in the fun, and Paul, who knows me well, gently makes fun of my decision; Paul—who sometimes forcibly holds me back, locking both of us in the bathroom if necessary, just to excite my impatience to mingle in the melee of bodies—promises to send me a friend of his that I have not yet met, someone who has nothing to do with the art world, a car mechanic. He knows that I would rather meet this man than go to the restaurant with the others and sit wearily on a terrace or in the corner of a nightclub waiting for the same weariness to overcome the rest of them. I don't pay much attention to Paul's proposition and look forward to an evening alone. There is something delicious about those moments when the emptiness around you opens up not only the space around you but also, somehow, the enormity of the time ahead. With unconscious economy, we make the most of this given opportunity by lazily settling into the depths of an armchair as if to leave as much space as possible to the onrush of time. The kitchen is right at the back of the villa, and I go and make myself a sandwich. My mouth is full when Paul's friend appears in the doorway that leads out to the garden. He is tall and dark with pale eyes, quite impressive in the darkness. He apologizes amicably, he can see that I'm eating, begs me not to stop just because of him . . . I am ashamed of the crumbs in the corners of my mouth. I say no, no, I'm not really hungry, and I chuck the sandwich away furtively.

He takes me away. He drives his convertible along the Grande Corniche above Nice. He takes one hand off the steering wheel to reply to mine rubbing against the rough surface of the bulge in his jeans. That swelling, impeded by the tight, stiff fabric, is an effective stimulus for me every time. Do I want to go and eat somewhere? No. I think he's driving a bit farther than he needs to, taking detours before getting home. He keeps his eyes on the road as I undo his belt. I recognize that little forward movement of the driver's hips that makes it easier to undo his zipper. Then there is the laborious process of extricating the member, which has grown too big to slip straight out of the double envelope of cotton. You need to have a wide enough hand to gather up all the parts in one smooth gesture. I am always afraid of hurting it. He has to help me. At last I can get on with my conscientious stroking. I never start too quickly, I really prefer following all its length, feeling the elasticity of the fine sheath of flesh. I put my mouth to it. I try to hold my body as far aside as possible, so as not to be in his way when he changes gear. I keep to a moderate rhythm. I am conscious of the danger that driving in these conditions could represent, and as a result, have no inclination to court it.

As far as I can remember, it was a very pleasant encounter. Even so, I didn't want to stay the night with him, and he had to take me back to the villa before the group got back. It was not that I had forbidden myself to stay out all night, but that I wanted the time I had spent with him to stay as it was (like when your thoughts wander off into a daydream halfway through a conversation), a private place to which the others, for once, would not have access.

...

The reader will have realized that, as I have explained, I exercised complete free will in my chosen sexual life, and if I orchestrated little breakaways, as I have just illustrated, this latitude could be measured only in terms of its direct opposite: the way fate brings people together, the determinism of the chain in which one link—one man—holds you to another, which links you to a third and so on. Mine was not the kind of freedom played out on the whims of circumstance; it was a freedom expressed once and for all, accepting the unreserved abandonment of the self to a way of life (like a nun saying her vows!). I have never formed a relationship—however fleeting—with someone I have met on a train or in the Métro, even though I have often heard stories of feverishly erotic encounters in such places, not to mention in elevators or restaurant bathrooms. I have always cut them short, rather abruptly even. I discourage them, humorously and gently, I hope, but in such an offhand way that it must look like firm resolution. Engaging myself in the playful meanderings of seduction and, however briefly, keeping up the teasing banter that necessarily occupies the interval between a chance meeting and accomplishing the sexual act would be beyond me. On the other hand, if it were possible for the thronging crowds at a train station or the organized hordes in the Métro to accept the crudest accesses of pleasure in their midst as they accept displays of the most abject misery, I could easily undertake that sort of coupling, like an animal.

Neither do I belong to the category of women who are "looking for adventure"; I have been successfully chatted up very rarely, and then never by strangers. On the other hand,

I have willingly accepted dates over the telephone from a voice, purporting to have met me at some function or another, to which I could not put a face. I was easy to find; they just had to call the magazine.

That was how I ended up at the opera one night, at a performance of *La Bohème*. I arrived late and had to wait till the end of the first scene before I could go and sit down in the darkness next to my virtual stranger. We had met, if you could call it that, a few days earlier at a mutual friend's party (when the relationship returns to the realm of a possible one-on-one, men rarely use the term "orgy"), but the profile I could see, the balding head and the jowly face, didn't mean a thing to me. I suspected that he had indeed been at the party but had not approached me there. He risked putting a hand on my thigh, looking at me furtively with something approaching anxiety. He never shook off his air of weariness; he had a habit of rubbing his head in the same way that he ran his great bony hands over me, doing it mechanically and complaining of terrible headaches. I thought he had a screw loose, and there was something rather pitiful about him. I saw him several more times; he took me to shows and to very expensive restaurants that I found more than a little entertaining, not because I could be mistaken for a prostitute but because I could outwit the ushers, the waitresses and the bourgeois patrons around us, given that the bald gentleman with the drooping skin was in conversation with a card-carrying intellectual.

To this day, Hortense (the switchboard operator at *Art Press*) sometimes puts through someone whose name I don't recognize. "They won't take no for an answer, they say they know you well." I take the call. From their carefully chosen words spoken in conspiratorial tones, I quickly realize that the stranger thinks he is talking to a real good-time girl, the sort, if I'm not mistaken, who leaves a man with some very good memories. (Similarly, if I am introduced to someone at a private opening or a dinner, and I feel that I am meeting him for the first time but he delves his eyes into mine for rather longer than is necessary, saying, "But we've already met," I tend to think that, in what feels like another life for me, he had an opportunity to look at my face at leisure while my gaze may have been locked on his pubic hair). I may no longer have the curiosity to take it any further, but I still have a profound admiration and sympathy for the suspension in time in which lovers live. It could be ten years, even twenty or more, since a man has made love to a woman, but he still talks about it and addresses her as if it were yesterday. Their pleasure is like a hardy perennial that knows no seasons. It flourishes in a greenhouse, isolated from outside contingencies so that they always see the body they held in the same way, even if it is now withered or lying stiffly in a robe. Be that as it may, experience has taught me that they cannot deny the principle of reality when it hits them in the face. If I don't warm to the telephone conversation, they inevitably ask a question, like a password that may or may not open the door. For example: "Are you married now?" "Yes." "Lovely, well, I'll give you a call next time I'm in Paris and perhaps we'll have a chance to see each other." I know I will never hear from them again.

...

To go back to those preliminaries that many women claim are the most delicious phase of a relationship, and which I have always tried to keep as brief as possible, I should make it clear that I have experienced them—and even then without prolonging them—in only two specific situations: when desire was already and unwittingly a breakaway faction of a profound and loving relationship; and after a relatively long period of abstinence, which amounts to exceptional circumstances.

In the latter case the signs were: an unexpected and frustrating sitting for a photographic portrait because—needless to say—the lighting was never quite right; a ride up in a elevator that was about as chatty as a funeral vigil; tiny, furtive kisses, then sneaky bites sneaked along the top of my bare arm when I had to place it on top of the layout table . . . I inhaled these libidinous effluvia rather like an asthmatic who unwisely strayed into a stifling hothouse. Very aware that I had done nothing to cultivate this sort of feeling in the past, I put them down to a sort of gentrification of my erotic life.

The other case proves that the sharpest of our sensual experiences can forge a path even through our least sensitive points of access. Even though I have no ear at all, and I go to the opera only for reasons that have nothing to do with the art of music, it is thanks to his voice that Jacques first appeared on the horizons of the vast plain of my desire. And yet his voice does not correspond to the sexy stereotype, it is neither velvet nor gravelly. Someone had recorded him reading a text and then played the tape to me over the telephone. I can still feel the echo it sent through me, radiating out to the most highly receptive point on my body. I gave myself over entirely to this voice, which itself seemed to give up entirely every detail of its speaker, a voice with the clarity and the calm rhythm of its brief inflections, as firm and assured as a hand turning up its palm to mean "There you have it." Sometime later I heard it on the telephone again, live this time, pointing out a typo in an exhibition catalog in which Jacques had been involved and on which I was working. He offered to come and help me correct the copies. We spent hours on the work, inches away from each other in a tiny office, with me very embarrassed by my mistake while he just got down to correcting it. He was attentive without being especially friendly. After one of these tedious sessions, he asked whether I would like to join him for dinner at a close friend's home. When dinner was over and several of us were squeezed next to one another on a bed serving as a sofa (which meant adopting an uncomfortable, semiprone position), Jacques stroked my wrist with the back of his index finger. It was an unexpected, unusual and quite delicious gesture, and it still moves me now, even when it is addressed to other skin than mine. I followed Jacques to the studio he was living in at the time. In the morning he asked me who I was sleeping with. "With lots of people," I replied. "Damn," he said, "I'm beginning to fall in love with a girl who's sleeping with lots of people."

The Pleasure of Telling

I have never tried to hide the extent or the eclectic variety of my sexual contacts, other than from my parents. (When I was a child and a "wedding night" was just a vague formula, even imagining that my mother would be able to picture me on that first night was truly a source of torment.) I have gradually and obscurely come to understand what this lifestyle had to offer me: the illusion of opening myself to innumerable possibilities. Given that I obviously had to comply with all sorts of constraints (a very demanding and stressful job, an upbringing defined by poverty and, the worst shackle of all, the baggage of family conflicts and rows in relationships), the certainty that I could have sexual relations in any situation with any willing party (as a matter of principle, the illusion held only on condition that anyone unwilling was excluded from the horizon) was the lungfuls of fresh air you inhale as you walk to the end of a narrow pier. And, as reality did still impose limits on this freedom (I couldn't do *only* that, and even if I could, the bracelet of my thighs could link together only a tiny part of the human chain), this meant that the spoken word, the briefest evocation of episodes in my sexual life, should always conjure up the panorama of possibilities in all their fullness. "I am here, with you, but if I talk about it, I pull aside the sheet, I open up a breach in the wall, and I let in the entire army of lovers that surrounds us." Usually, after about the third or fourth date, I would drop in a few men's names, connecting them with day-to-day activities that were, nonetheless, open to ambiguous interpretation, and— if I was feeling more confident—I might refer to a few picturesque situations in which I had made love in the past. I would evaluate the reaction.

I have said that I did not go in for preaching, and even less for provocation, except as part of a well-meaning and harmless perversion, addressed only to people who had already been identified as kindred spirits. I was careful to be sincere, adhering to a dialectic with three terms: to some extent I protected myself from new relationships by branching out only if there was a connection with my community of swingers; in doing this I could identify whether or not the newcomer belonged to this community; finally, whatever his reaction, while still taking care to protect myself, I would appeal to his curiosity.

The friend who made me speak so much while we were fornicating insisted that, as well as evoking fantasies, I should talk about things that had really happened—as it should be. I had to give names, describe places and say exactly how many times. If I failed to specify when describing a new acquaintance, he was quick to ask: "Did you sleep with him?" But his interest did not focus exclusively on an obscene inventory ("What color was his glans when you drew back his foreskin? Brown? Red? Did you give him one up the ass? With your tongue? Or your fingers? How many fingers did you stick up his ass?"), it also extended to the more banal aspects of the setting: "We were visiting an apartment for rent in the rue Beaubourg, the carpet had balls of fluff all over it and he took me there and then on a mattress on the floor." "He's a bouncer for *The Johnny Halliday Show;* that's how I saw the whole show from the side of the stage, it felt as if the speakers were inside me. We came home on his Harley Davidson; it didn't have any backseat left, and the frame was carving into my pussy; when we did eventually fuck, I was already spliced open like a ripe grapefruit." A basic sentimentality was always welcome: "Was he in love with you?" Me: "Hmm." Him: "I'm sure he's in love with you." Me: "The other morning I was pretending to sleep, and I heard him whispering, 'I love you,

Catherine; I love you, Catherine,' and these breathy words were accompanied by a little movement of his belly, not as if he was fucking but more like a big cat twitching in its sleep." A sentimentality corrupted by the jealousy of a third party: "Does he know you fuck everyone in town? He's jealous, isn't he?" The antics of another friend of mine who fucked me laid out on his worktable, right in the middle of his high-tech art studio, while presenting his dick like a monstrous pistil emerging from the corolla of ephemeral, crotchless women's panties—a baroque touch in that austere setting—particularly appealed to him. I had to narrate it dozens of times, not even having to embellish it with variations, and even after I had stopped seeing the other friend. If I could come quickly while masturbating that morning when I woke up, or in the office, in such and such a position and having made myself come X number of times in succession, that worked, too. I never invented an adventure that hadn't happened, and my descriptions betrayed reality no more than any transposition inevitably does. As I have already pointed out, the realm of fantasy and the realm of experience may well be close neighbors, but to me, they are still independent of each other, like a landscape painting and the corner of the countryside that it actually represents; there is more of the artist's interior vision than reality in the painting. The fact that, from then on, we see that reality through the prism of the painting does not stop the trees from growing or their leaves from dropping. It is not unusual, at an orgy, for a man occupying a pussy that has already been well reconnoitered to worry about the effect his predecessors may have had. "You were crying out earlier. Tell me about it. He has a big cock, doesn't he? He must have really had to ram it in, and you liked it. You were behaving like a woman in love. Don't deny it, I saw you." I have to admit that sometimes, contrary to expectations, I would reply honestly—no, I liked his cock just as much—because at the time I hadn't learned to correct my scrupulous instincts, but also because of my writerly unwillingness to repeat myself.

But usually this chronicling of events took place outside of carnal exchanges. In that instance, the words hang in the space between those who are speaking, like a house of cards built up by their play of questions and answers, and which they hope won't suddenly crumble in the face of prematurely salacious confessions or a curiosity that too quickly becomes indiscreet. While driving in his falling-apart little car, one friend asked me almost curtly: How old were you when you started swinging? What sort of people did you meet at orgies—middle-class types? Were there lots of girls? How many men fucked you in one evening? Did you come every time? My replies were equally matter-of-fact. At one point he pulled over, not so that we could touch each other but to pursue the interrogation, his face quite relaxed, his eyes focused well beyond the end of the street. Did I take several at the same time, in my pussy and in my mouth? "That's the best, and jerking off two more with my hands." This particular friend was a journalist; he ended up interviewing me for a magazine he contributed to.

In my immediate circle of friends, it was a question of keeping the excitement at a certain level verbally so that all the members of the club could clandestinely identify one another anywhere, at a work-related meeting or at a party, and could tolerate the conformist nature of the event, for example at a housewarming party where there are lots of guests. They come and go in the artist's huge at-home studio and there isn't anywhere to sit. "Is that guy there the one you have such a fantastic time with? That's great; he's not much to look at, but that doesn't mean anything. What the hell does he do to you?" I reply with a nod of the head; it's true that he's ugly, and more than that, he's out of place here. In my wanderings I come across lots of different kinds of people, and I like arranging for these worlds to meet. I made sure he was invited even though they didn't know him. Someone comes and asks me who the guy is in the hopelessly outdated hippie smock. All the same . . . When I spend the night with him, our bodies tangled up on his bed, we suck each other off for hours. During a sixty-nine, it really gets me going to rub my breasts against a slightly rubbery tummy. "It's true, you seem to go for chubby ones." Me: "I dreamed I met François Mitterand at an orgy! . . . and I like them not that clean, too . . . I'm pretty sure he never brushes his teeth." "You're disgusting. He's married, isn't he?" Me: "I've seen a picture of his wife. So ugly you wouldn't believe it."

That gets me going, too. My voice is no louder than usual, but I give details only sparingly. I take pleasure in evoking this dirtiness and this contagious ugliness, at the same time savoring the disgust of the man questioning me. "You suck each other. And then?" Me: "You can't imagine the way he moans when I lick his ass . . . he gets in the doggie position, his ass is so white . . . he wriggles it when I burrow my nose into it. Then I get onto all fours . . . he finishes quickly, with short little thrusts that are—how shall I put this—very precise." The man I'm talking to is part of the scene, too, but I've never happened to sleep with him. I'm not especially attracted to him, either. The man I'm referring to is not the sort to assail me with questions, but he listens to me, and in the end, because everyone ends up calling their friends' friends by their first names even if they haven't met them themselves, I think of him as part of the group.

The more sociable I became, the better I cultivated my innate pragmatism in all aspects of sexual exchanges. Having, in the early days, tested various partners' receptivity to ménages à trois, I adapted the words I used. A faint, decadent aura around me was enough for some, whereas others, as I have illustrated, wanted to enjoy by proxy every last fingering. Added to this is the fact that even the most truthful speech is obviously never absolute, is always colored by the way feelings have evolved. I was very talkative with Jacques at first, but then I had to cope, more or less well and anyway belatedly, with the ban imposed on sexual adventures and accounts of these adventures the moment our relationship was perceived and lived as one of love, even though more than once, I read descriptions of erotic scenes in Jacques's books that could only have been reworkings of anecdotes I had told him. Of all the men I saw for any length of time, only two brought my exhaustive exposés to an abrupt halt. And even then I am pretty sure that these details they didn't want to know, and which were therefore not mentioned, still formed a central part of our exchanges.

...

Those who obey social mores are probably better equipped to confront demonstrations of jealousy than those with a libertine philosophy that leaves them feeling helpless in the face of passion. A person can prove her extensive and sincere liberality by sharing the pleasure she takes with the person she most loves, only for it to be pierced, without any warning, by an exactly proportionate intolerance. Jealousy may have been bubbling within like a spring, and as the bubbles burst it might even have been giving a regular and subterranean form of irrigation to the garden of libido, until—suddenly—it formed a torrent and then the entire conscious mind was submerged by it, as has been described by so many people.

I have learned this from observation as well as from experience. I personally have experienced my confrontations with these passionate expressions of jealousy in a sort of stupor that even the brutal death of a loved one did not provoke. And I had to read Victor Hugo, yes, I had to go and seek out that portrayal of God the Father, to understand that this stupor is comparable to the sort of denial displayed by children. "To accept facts as they are does not belong to realms of childhood. [A child forms] impressions as his terror grows but without making any connection between the two and without drawing any conclusions," I once read in *The Man Who Laughs,* finally finding an explanation for my mindless inertia. And I can confirm that, even after you have done all the growing you should do, you can still experience what I would describe as an incomprehension of injustice that prevents you from seeing the feelings behind the injustice. I was once beaten all the way along the path that runs from the rue

Las Cases toward the area around the church of Notre-Dame-des-Champs, beaten and trampled in the gutter and, when I got back to my feet, forced to walk through a series of punches to the back of my neck and my shoulders, the way they used to drive common thieves to the dungeons. We had just left a party that hadn't come close to an orgy but had at one point been enlivened by a sort of conga around the apartment, during which a fairly prominent man had taken advantage of our passage through the dimly lit sitting room to push me onto a sofa and drench my ear with his saliva. And yet the friend who beat me had already come with me to other parties with much more absolute ends. When, later that night, I retraced our steps all the way up the path, in the vain hope of finding a piece of jewelry that had fallen off under his blows, my thoughts were focused exclusively on this specific loss. On another occasion, one of my unwisely detailed accounts earned me a less furious—although equally aggressive—revenge: a slash with a razor on my right shoulder while I lay sleeping on my belly, but not before the blade had been carefully disinfected on a burner in the kitchen. The scar, which I still have, is shaped like a stupid little mouth, a good illustration of what I felt at the time.

My own jealousy has been episodic. If I have used my sexual itinerary to satisfy my intellectual and professional curiosity, I have nevertheless remained perfectly indifferent to my friends' love lives and marriages. It goes even beyond indifference, perhaps contempt. I have had rushes of jealousy only with the men I have lived with and then, oddly, on a quite different basis in both cases. It pained me every time Claude was seduced by a woman whom I judged to be prettier than myself. I am not ugly, but only if you take my appearance as a whole; there's nothing remarkable about my features. It galled me that I couldn't enhance my sexual performances—which, in principle, had no limitations—with a physical appearance that, itself, could not be improved. I really would have loved it if I, the girl who gave the best blow job, the one who was always first to get going at an orgy, hadn't been short, with eyes that are slightly too close together, a long nose, etc. I could describe in great detail the physical traits that attracted Claude: a triangular face and the hairstyle of one of the secretaries whose slender torso provided a contrast to set off her rounded shoulders and conical breasts; the pale-colored eyes of another woman, who had brown hair, like mine; the smooth temples and doll-like cheeks of a third. It goes without saying that such a powerful contradiction to the principles of sexual freedom meant that this agony could not be articulated and, therefore, reduced me to scenes and crying fits that were all the more intractable, and fits of hysteria worthy of Paul Richer's *L'arc hystérique*.

With Jacques, my jealousy took the form of a terrible feeling of being supplanted. The images I could dream up, of some woman whose haunches, while I was away, would obscure the tip of his sex from view, in a setting that was familiar to us, or whose whole enormous, ever expanding body inhabited the smallest part of our environment—the running board of the car, the leafy design of a sofa cover, the side of the sink you lean your belly on when you rinse out a cup—who might even have left strands of her hair inside my motorbike helmet, these images caused me such acute pain that I had to escape them with the most drastic fantasizing. I would imagine that, having caught them in the act, I would leave the house, set off along the boulevard Diderot toward the Seine, which wasn't far away, and throw myself in. Or I would go on walking to the point of exhaustion and be taken to the hospital, speechless and out of my wits.

Another, less pathetic, escape route consisted in intensive masturbatory activity. As I have already begun to disclose the sort of narratives that sustain this activity, it might be interesting if I said something about the modifications they undergo at a given point. My wanderings over wasteland and the delivery-boy characters, taking advantage of the situation phlegmatically, were replaced by a limited repertoire of scenes in which I no longer appeared and Jacques was the only male figure, accompanied by one or other of his girlfriends. The scenes would be partly imaginary, partly constructed from snippets harvested by trespassing into Jacques's notebooks or his letters, because he's not very talkative on the subject. Cramped in an Austin parked under a railway bridge, he keeps her head down on his belly, holding it carefully with both hands as if manipulating the glass dome that houses a precious object, until his come has spurted into the back of her throat and he has heard the gulp as she swallows reticently. Or a big white backside exposed on the sofa in the sitting room like a gigantic mushroom, and Jacques sinking into it as he spanks it smartly. Another option is for the girl to be standing with one foot up on a stool, in the position some women adopt to insert a tampon; Jacques, hanging on to her hips and braced on his tiptoes, penetrates her in the same configuration: from behind. I would consistently orgasm at the point in my narrative when I allowed Jacques to ejaculate, when

the watchful eye in my mind recognized that powerful asym-
metrical contraction of his face. This confiscation of my old
fantasies eventually produced a defensive reaction, but I still
needed considerable perseverance and force of will for the
sequences in which I was the protagonist to take back that
zone of my imagination.

...

I cannot close this chapter on exchange (which, like a silk
worm's cocoon, covers and constitutes the sexual relationships) without bringing up my only failed attempt at prosti-
tution. When I heard mention of Madame Claude, I would
always succumb to fanciful daydreams about high-class pros-
titution, envying Catherine Deneuve's character in *Belle de
jour,* but I would have been completely incapable of negoti-
ating the least exchange of this sort. People used to say that
Lydie, the only woman I knew who was as aggressive as a man
during an orgy, had spent several days in a brothel in Palermo,
earning enough money to throw a fantastic party for one of
her friends. There was something mythical about this to me,
and it left me stunned. I have made enough references to my
shyness, to my excessive reserve, for the reasons to be clear.
To establish a mercenary relationship, you have to navigate
an exchange of words or at least signals, the sort of complicity that forms the basis for all conversations and which would
have seemed, to me, closely related to the preliminaries of
seduction that I avoided. In both cases, in order to keep to
your side of the deal, you have to take into account your
partner's attitudes and responses. Now, even at the first con-

tact, I knew only how to focus on the body. It is just when I have found my bearings with the body, as it were, when the grain of the skin and its particular pigmentation have become familiar to me, or I have learned to adjust my own body to it, that my attention could focus on the person himself, often to form a sincere and lasting friendship. But by then it would no longer be right to ask for money.

Still, I really needed it. An old school friend wanted to help me out. A contact of hers had asked whether she would like to meet a woman who was keen to be introduced to very young women. She did not dare go herself but thought that I might be interested. My friend had an idea that doing such a thing with a woman was less "consequential" than with a man. I was given a rendezvous time in a café in Montparnasse, with a suspicious go-between, a man of about thirty-five who looked like a real estate agent. As a precaution, a friend watched me from a distance. I don't remember anything about the conversation or the proposed arrangements; I seem to recall the guy was very careful to describe the woman we were meant to be meeting, while I, probably unable to imagine myself cast as a prostitute, switched the roles in my mind's eye and imagined this woman as an aging call girl, with bleached hair and lingerie that sagged on her flesh, lying back on a furry bedcover with silent authority. Despite my naïveté, I realized as soon as the man took me to one of the little hotels I knew on the rue Jules-Chaplain that I would never see the woman. Perhaps the fact that he had spoken about her so much had immediately and definitively sent her back to the realms of imagination. The room was pleasantly cozy; he switched on both bedside lights without bothering to switch off the overhead light, undid his zipper straightaway and asked me to suck him, in the same tone of voice as a man apologizing for bumping into you on the Métro even though he seems to think it's your fault. I carried out the job, only too relieved that I no longer had to face his rudeness. He lay down on the satin bedcover, he had a good hard erection and was easy to handle. I sucked him steadily without tiring, resting squarely on my knees, which were perpendicular to his hips—one of the most comfortable positions. I was keen to finish because my thoughts were spinning. Should I say anything more about the woman we were meant to be meeting? That would be stupid. Should I ask for money for the blow job? But shouldn't I have done that first? What was I going to tell the friend waiting for me? I was surprised by the sincere and youthful, abandoned expression on his face when he came, it was such a contrast to the way he behaved; it was also the only time in my life that I saw our pleasure of a man I didn't like. I still have a clear image of the room as it was when we left it, the immaculate bedspread, the untouched chairs and the uncluttered surfaces of the little bedside tables under the lamp shades. I denied it, but I could not disguise from the attentive friend who met me on a nearby terrace that I had made extensive use of my mouth. A blow job, especially if it is well done, bruises the insides of the lips. If you keep on going back and forth with your mouth, it's better to protect the aroused member by curling your lips over your teeth—at least that's the way I have always proceeded. "Your lips are all swollen," said my friend, telling me I was a fool. The young man who looked like a real estate agent had followed me. He insulted us, claiming we had tried to con him in some way. I couldn't quite see how, but luckily he didn't press the point.

What teasing I have had for offering my body so easily but not knowing how to make money from it! I was with men who were relatively well off, but I wasn't the type to put on the sort of performance that would have been necessary to gain any material advantage from them—advantages that they doubtless conferred on other girls. If I had to make a list, like a head of state who has to keep records of gifts received from ambassadors or foreign heads of state, the spoils would be meager: a pair of sparkly orange stockings I have never worn; three thick 1930s bangles in Bakelite; a pair of off-white knitted shorts (definitely one of the first styles to come out in the winter 1970 prêt-à-porter collection) with a matching top; an authentic Berber wedding dress; a dime-store watch; a plastic brooch with a baroque geometric design typical of the early eighties; a necklace and a ring by Zolotas, which, sadly, tarnished very quickly; a pearl-edged pareo; a Japanese-brand vibrating dildo, along with three little metallic balls meant to be inserted in the vagina to stimulate you during the act, which never worked for me . . . I should also add a contribution to the first dress I ever bought from a YSL boutique; a bath towel, also from YSL; extensive free dental care; and a loan of several thousand francs that I never had to repay. Taxis and airfare have always been paid for. "You looked lost," someone who knew me when I was very young tells me, "and people just couldn't help themselves giving you hundred-franc notes." I must have gone on looking like that to men all my life, not like a woman who was after money, far from it, but like an adolescent who was no good at earning her living and needed help with a little allowance. I have, of course, excluded from this list all the presents Jacques gave me, given that our relationship was of a different order, and I also separate the works given to me by artists, because I always think—as, indeed, I do every time my professional interests have been closely linked with my sexual relationships—that they gratify the art critic in me just as much as, when that is their intention, they do the lover.

Always First Times

We do not stick to the same sexual diet all the way through our lives! This may be due to our emotional circumstances (all our desires may be channeled through one person) but also to those times when we take stock of ourselves, thanks to changes that may have intervened in aspects of our lives not necessarily connected with love (moving, illness, a new professional or intellectual environment), when we find ourselves off the track we were following.

I can think of two occasions when my libido was stalled. When Jacques and I were preparing to live together, he wrote to tell me that we should hide absolutely nothing from each other, that we shouldn't lie. Now, it just happened that I had formed some relationships that I thought he wouldn't be happy about. I managed to avoid a couple of meetings, to stagger my visits to orgies and to go through with the rest in a guilty state that I had hardly ever experienced and which had an inhibiting effect, moderate but nonetheless real. On the other hand, one particular orgy, which was in no way extraordinary, marked a turning point for me. I knew the couple who were our hosts, and—because he had just taken on the

73

management of a big newspaper and she was a singer—I thought of them as parodies of characters from *Citizen Kane*. I had already fucked if not both of them, certainly him. There were some distinguished guests, and they had split into two groups: one in a bedroom, the other on a sofa that stood rather oddly in the middle of a living-room, lit by a chandelier. I was on the sofa, definitely glad to be in the group that was better lit, and active as I always was. I rather liked our host's dick, a short sturdy organ whose proportions made it a reduced model of his entire, compact body. Some people started to head for the bedroom, where a young woman buried in a thick down comforter and waving her limbs in the air like a baby in its crib was hidden under the succession of broad backs that came and covered her, and whose cries could be heard all over the apartment. I observe this sort of extroverted behavior with placid indifference. One of the participants expressed his admiration, saying she was "really going for it," and I thought this was stupid. I went back to relax on the sofa. I thought that this young woman had taken up center stage, which, till then, had been mine, and that I should have been jealous of her, but my jealousy was lukewarm. For the first time ever, I was pausing during one of those sessions in which I normally kept it up without stopping. And I appreciated that pause in the same way as I valued those moments when I withdrew into myself during a meal or while out with friends. Of course, I wondered about this new reaction. The answer I found was that by constantly talking openly about these sort of practices with people who did or did not perform them; by commenting on them and interpreting them, usually with the arsenal of lay psychoanalysis (which had the same effect on me as a cavalry regiment descending on an encampment of rebel Indians); in short, by heading to a couch three times a week not to fuck but to talk about it, I had—without realizing it—taken on the role not only of an active participant but also of an observer.

And it was when I moved away from the center of the spiral that I discovered something: my pleasure was never more intense than when it was the first time—not the first time that I made love with someone, but the first time we kissed; even the first embrace was enough. Obviously there were exceptions. Be that as it may, in most cases, even if what followed was not unpleasant, it was a bit like biting into the cone when you no longer have a mouthful of ice cream to melt on your tongue; it had all the attraction of a painting that you admire but on which you are feasting your eyes for the fifteenth time. If I was taken by surprise, the pleasure was overwhelming. It is these situations that provide some of my clearest recollections of orgasms. I can cite them: late at night, crossing the huge lobby of an Inter-Continental hotel; the elegant and distinguished assistant who has been traveling across the country with me for more than two weeks catches hold of my arm after we have just said goodnight to each other, pulls me to him and kisses me on the mouth. "In the morning, I'll come and see you in your room." I can feel the spasm rising right up to my stomach, and I set off toward the tiny little concierge's desk in the distance, twisting my ankle as I go.

Another time, I dive down onto the carpet next to the master of the house, who, slightly drunk, has crashed out on the floor next to some other guests, and who pulls me toward him by tugging under the neck of my sweater, kissing me slowly with one of those cinema kisses that makes your head roll from side to side; this was not an evening destined to turn into an orgy, his wife was holding a conversation in the next room. One of his friends who was also sitting on the floor like us and whose face happened to be on a level with ours, watched us in amazement. I go completely limp.

And more: going to see the "Dernier Picasso" exhibition at the Pompidou Center with Bruno, with him there is always an element of chance. As he goes out of my field of vision while I go up to one of the paintings, his presence becomes all the more vivid and I am caught unaware by a brief but very distinct wetness between my legs. As I keep looking at the exhibition, I can feel the slimy patch on my tights alternately against the lips of my vagina and the swell of my inner thigh, shifting as I walk. In an early period of my life, I didn't really care whether I reexperienced these feelings in more extensive caresses or during penetration, but later on, when I had come to understand how singularly limited it was, I started to hope that that faraway, ineffable tension in my lower abdomen, and the famous wave that dissipated it, could be repeated again and again as a relationship continued.

...

As I approached middle age, I had two successive relationships, one easygoing and the other emotionally charged, but nevertheless they both followed a similar pattern: I took the time to let the desire I felt for the other soak in, which made that desire all the more pronounced; it culminated in passionate bouts of fucking during which my satisfaction was never as complete as it had been in the inaugural physical contact. For many years I faithfully maintained a friendship with Bruno, but it was threatened periodically by bursts of desire, sometimes aggressive, frustrated, not satisfactorily fulfilled, etc. It was my only truly chaotic experience. I would go to see him every day for weeks on end, then one day I would ring the doorbell and there would be no reply; the door would stay closed for several weeks, months even. And this would go on until my incredulous persistence was at last rewarded by a hoarse interjection on the telephone, authorizing me to come see him once again. Probably because of this climate of uncertainty, I often came instantly to orgasm with him. We would talk volubly, exchanging impressions of books, usually standing in a sparse interior that would have made a Quaker feel at home. Time would pass and I would move toward him. "Do we want a little cuddle?" he would ask in the preoccupied but affectionate voice of an adult disturbed in his work by a child. Then his hand would push aside my panties, and two fingers, four, would elicit a brief, anguished cry from me, because it was as much a sensation of breathtaking surprise as of pleasure. He himself would have the satisfaction of knowing that my pussy was already dripping. We were generous with our kisses and caresses. He made sweeping movements. If I was lying down, he would brush aside the sheet with the same gesture that he used to stroke my breasts throughout; I could lie straight and motionless on my back while his palm swept up and down my entire length, as if I was just a sketch. When it was my turn to attend to him, in contrast I explored him minutely, paying special attention to the folds in his body, behind the ear, his groin, his armpits, the crack between his buttocks. I even scoured the furrowed lines in the crook of his hands. Throughout these preliminaries, I kept thinking how delicious it would be later on when he made up his mind to turn me over and take me the way I like it, from behind, when he grabbed my buttocks and smacked into them loudly and abruptly with his hips. I particularly like it when the dick jerks in and out; every three or four pumps, a slightly harder thrust comes as a glorious surprise. And yet it was only on a few exceptional occasions that I felt the same intense pleasure as when his fingers opened up the way. So I would start thinking that perhaps the next time I would, and I settled in to wait, occupying myself with the need to force the resistance of that closed door or the moral lesson.

Before that, I had a relationship with the author of the failed photographs taken in my office. He would arrange to meet me either in a hotel near Gobelins or in a disused apartment near the Gare de l'Est that was on loan to him. These meetings were always at an ungodly hour for anyone trying to carry on professional activities that were just a tad dependent on office hours: between eleven o'clock and midday, between half past three and four o'clock in the afternoon . . . The day before, I could already feel the anticipation in my pussy responding to the vibrating Métro seat while I looked forward to our reunion. The feeling could be so maddening that I sometimes preferred to get off a few stops before my destination, to calm myself down by walking. That man could lick my snatch indefinitely. His tongue moved languorously, diligently parting all the folds of the vulva, knowingly describing circles round the clitoris then licking broadly like a young dog over the opening. The need to feel his sex breaching that gap became imperative. When at last he penetrated me, just as softly and delving just as meticulously as he had with his tongue, my pleasure never managed to measure up to the escalation of desire.

Given the journeys I had to make to get to these rendezvous in only a short space of time, we sometimes missed each other. If he didn't turn up, I would stay lying on the bed, swinging my legs, my wanting wedged painfully between my legs, stopping me from closing them like a crossbar. Afterward I felt a seemingly insurmountable oppression that stopped me from completing the day's tasks, going back to the office, making telephone calls or even the simplest decisions. How could I live a normal life until the next time we met, as if things were just fine? My gaping desire made me feel like an abandoned wooden puppet, its stiff wooden legs spread helplessly, unable to move of their own free will. But happily, this debilitation, which always hovers over me and varies in obsessiveness according to the situation, does not last. Even though I never consciously decide that it should be, the door of my office is always a perfectly impermeable screen, and I may well be dripping wet between the legs (or could have been through any kind of event), I have the happy gift of being able to throw myself into my work with the same facility.

...

Would I ever have thought of writing this book, which opens with a chapter called "Numbers," if I had not once experienced being a minute satellite that suddenly left the orbit where it had been held by a whole network of connections that no longer governed it? The liftoff happened in two stages. First, there were times when I found satisfaction less frequently, and I coped with this frustration less tolerantly than I have just described. My excitement could rise to very high levels. The signs I took as precursors of an overwhelming pleasure were goose pimples and my lips turning cold (I will come back to these sensations in more detail later). If, as had more frequently become the case, the process ground to a halt, I would feel like an insurmountable obstacle towered in front of me instead of the vast release I had hoped for. Each time, in the very moment when my partner was moving away and I was closing my legs, I searched, with the same stubborn resolve as when I am trying to describe something in an article, for a definition of the feelings inside me that I could not put into words. What name should I give to this singular emotion? That was the question I put to myself. It was, I'm sure, a loathing of whoever was next to me at the time, but one obviously independent of my feelings for him the rest of the time. But at that moment this loathing filled me as closely and as fully as a liquid metal occupies a mold. I struggled obstinately to describe it to myself, and I remember sometimes comparing it to another form of sculpture: Tony Smith's hermetic *Die*. Luckily, like the oppression that came over me after a failed rendezvous but never lasted beyond the trip back in the taxi or the Métro, this lacerating hatred put up no resistance to my reflex to slip off to the bathroom. And I think that it was in that position, as I ran a towel between my legs, that I first thought I ought to tell all about it.

For a period that I think lasted three years, perhaps four, and which constitutes what I think of as the second stage, my opportunities for sexual contact became rarer, and when they did arise, they were more or less like the frustrations described above. I also spent long weeks alone in Paris in the summer, my time divided between long working days and nights cut short both by the heat and by all the usual stress. That was when I delved through a pile of underwear and found the dildo I had been given years before and had never used. It had two different functions that could each be operated at two speeds. At one end there was a doll's head with a star on her forehead and a hairstyle that swept into wide curls around her neck, corresponding to the rolled edges of the glans. This head rotated in smaller or larger circles while something looking rather like a wild boar, attached halfway down the shaft, quivered its extremely long tongue (either quickly or slowly), intended for the clitoris. The first time I used the thing, I came instantly, in one very long, perfectly identifiable, measurable spasm, and without needing to fantasize. I was completely taken aback. So an orgasm—an orgasm of the purest quality, even—could be achieved without perpetually having to return to that wellspring, the thrill of the "first time," by recreating various first times, and without the time to convene my mental repertoire of delivery boys and workmen. I very often wept after these speedy sessions. They combined a painfully violent pleasure with that sensuous delight of being alone, here slightly heightened by a touch of bitterness. The contrast between something that corresponded so accurately with what is known as solitary pleasure and my usual taste for plurality was comic. One time I thought to myself that if I ever had to speak out about "the truth of the situation," the book should be called *The Sexual Life of Catherine M.* It made me laugh out loud all by myself.

...

Although poorly provided for by nature in the first place, I now have the benefit of very healthy teeth, thanks to an excellent dentist who never once sent me a bill. The first time that he greeted me as usual in his surgery and then showed me through to another waiting room, not the one where I usually waited, a bigger room furnished quite differently with antique and not modern furniture, it was a bizarre, disturbing experience; it was as if, by passing through a familiar doorway, I had been magically transported to a film set or into a dream. He left me there alone. Then burst into the room, pushed my clothes away from my breasts and my ass, caressed me and disappeared. Reappeared ten minutes later with a young woman. The three of us fucked. I understood only later that it was a double surgery with two waiting rooms leading to two adjoining treatment rooms. Julien went from one to the other, treating one patient while the dressings on another dried. If I (or one of his other girlfriends, or a combination of the two) was in one of the treatment rooms, he could, with tremendous sleight of hand, rev up his dick against one of our pussies, tidy it away, disappear through the connecting door, then nip back. He usually ejaculated when he had scarcely penetrated. He had designed and decorated this double surgery himself, working on it late into the evening after his last patients had left. At the weekend he competed in tennis tournaments at quite a high level. He would sometimes arrange to meet me in the afternoon, having booked a room in a grand hotel. I would check in, he would join me for fifteen minutes and leave me the money to check out. I was fond of him. I was touched by the mysterious force that drove him in his tireless activity. And I identified with him, to some extent, because I never stopped, and as soon as I was in one place I wanted to be somewhere else, to see what was on the other side of the wall.

On walks, I hate coming back the same way that I set out. I study maps in minute detail to find a new way of getting to some piece of countryside, an edifice or a curiosity I haven't yet seen. When I went to Australia, the farthest I could get from home on this earth, I realized that my perception of this distance could be compared to the concept of having no sexual barriers. While I was thinking about this, I wondered whether the joy of parenthood belonged to the same family of emotions. Éric's ideas were in the same vein; he so cleverly adapted and changed the form our evenings took in the same way that (and these are his words) a "tour guide" would. What mattered, he would point out, was to "widen the available space."

2. Space

Surely someone ought to write a study of the reasons why, during the course of their careers, eminent art historians (such as André Chastel and Giulio Carlo Argan) have focused increasingly on architecture. How did their analysis of the space represented in a painting mutate into an analysis of the way real space is organized? In my role as an art critic, I might have felt more inclined to follow their example if I had not come across modern and contemporary pictorial works that could be said to inhabit the cusp between imaginary space and the space we live in, be they Barnett Newman's vast colored expanses (Newman himself said: "I declare space"), the radiant blues in the work of Yves Klein (who called himself the "painter of space") or even Alain Jacquet's topological surfaces and objects which juxtapose paradoxical abysses. What characterizes these works is not the fact that they open space up, but that they both open and seal it again—Newman with his closing "zips," Klein by crushing his anthropometric forms, Jacquet by binding the ends of a Möbius strip. If you allow yourself to be led, it's like the boundless inner surface of a lung.

The Gates of Paris

The Porte de Saint-Cloud parking lot borders on the boulevard Périphérique and in places is separated from it only by an openwork wall. All I had on were my shoes, having slipped off my raincoat, whose lining iced my skin, before getting out of the car. At first, as I have said, they rammed me up against a perpendicular wall. Éric saw me "pinned up by their pricks, like a butterfly." Two men held me up under the arms and legs, while the others took it in turns hammering against the pelvis to which my whole person had been reduced. In these dicey situations, where there are many of them, men often fuck quickly and forcefully. I could feel the rugged surface of the breezeblocks digging into my shoulders and my hips. Even though it was late, there was still some traffic. The thrumming of the cars, so close they seemed to almost brush past us, lulled me into the same daze I feel at airports. With my body both freed of all weight and curled up on itself, I retreated within myself. From time to time I would glimpse through my half-closed eyes the headlights of a car as they swept over my face. The men moved away from the wall, and I felt myself being simultaneously levered up by two powerful jacks. A current fantasy, which had been nourishing my masturbation sessions for a long time, was to be taken to the dark foyer of a building by two strangers and to be impaled by both at the same time, like a sandwich, one in my cunt, the other up my ass, and here it found substance in an obscure atmosphere where reality and the images conjured in my mind fed off each other.

I must have come to, if I can call it that, when my body was returned to a more normal form of support. Someone threw a coat over the hood of a car, and they lay me down on it. I'm familiar with this position, which is not an easy one; I kept slipping, and there was nothing to hold on to. I didn't always respond well to the different cocks that sought out my wet, sticky canal. I was the focal point for a theater of shadows, invisible until headlights threw their insipid light over the scene. From there I could make out the group scattered far and wide about me; those who had already shot their load seemed to completely lose interest in the ensuing proceedings. In front of me was the silhouette of a much larger vehicle, probably a truck; perhaps it had been chosen as a makeshift screen.

I remember when we arrived at the little stadium at Vélizy-Villacoublay how funny it seemed. The trip there had been so long, the leader of the convoy so mysterious about the destination, that when we came upon the place, like a great clearing in the middle of a forest, it just made us burst out laughing. It was a clear night. When you go to so much trouble to find a place, it's usually for somewhere less exposed, more appropriate for complicity! On top of that, we all realized that we were going to be fornicating amid the ghosts of all the adolescents who came and played soccer there every Wednesday afternoon. Our guide responded to our questions by admitting that this had indeed been where he came for soccer practice. He looked crestfallen, as if he had been forced to admit to a long-standing fantasy. Who hasn't dreamed of polluting some ordinary and innocent place they know with a bit of hanky-panky? The group took refuge under the sloping terraces because it goes so against human nature to copulate in full view of the horizon or in too expansive a space. On the whole, we protect ourselves less from others' gazes, which can constitute an even more definite barrier than their bodies. People who fuck on the beach on moonlit summer nights think about the intimacy of their situation, and this cuts them off from the immensity around them. Our group was too big and too spread out to create that sort of intimacy. I took the cocks standing up, hanging on to some of the posts under the terraces, with my dress lifted up (I didn't want to take everything off because it was so cold, but my buttocks were still completely exposed). Because I have a very supple waist, I am well suited to this position. So this circle of joyful activity continued, forming a perimeter around my outstretched ass, while I gazed absently through the frame of floorboards to the empty field.

I think I must have ended up naked. There was some joke about the available changing rooms: might as well make the most of them. They were behind a little shed, which must have served as a concession stand as well because it had a counter along the front. I lay down there for a while, taking ambivalent pleasure in being manhandled and inspected like a choice piece of merchandise. I wriggled about and breathed deeply of the damp night air. The shed roof extended into an awning over the counter. The wooden walls were clean and smooth, with no notices pinned to them, the general impression simplicity bordering on minimalism, like those theater sets that designers dream up that are like working drawings, far removed from reality. I was treated to some final fondlings, to a few licks on my vulva offered at just the right height and then, as the journey there had been so long, the cars soon set off again.

Many of these adventures take place at night, and this is obviously because the public places that allow you to gather in large groups and that provide amusing stages (for spectacles for which they were never intended) are more accessible and are not usually as closely guarded. That is how one of Éric's girlfriends came to know the icy but stimulating sensation a huge belt buckle left on her buttocks when the couple and a group of bikers had arranged to meet in the Bois. People also think that darkness protects them. But for some people, me included, it simultaneously opens the space around them up to infinity by making it limitless. The tall hedge a few meters away is no longer an obstacle. In fact, you hardly ever find complete darkness, and people actually usually prefer the vagueness of half-light. I myself would like total blackout because I could then experience the pleasure of sinking into a sea of undifferentiated flesh. On the other hand, I know how to make the most of harsh light, too, because the initial blindness and inability to identify its source dissolve and blur the frontiers of the body. In other words, I am not afraid of being glimpsed unaware, because my body is but a mingling part of the air around it and the continuum of other bodies connected to it. I therefore can't even conceive that anyone is looking in from the outside.

When Bruno and I were out for a walk after dinner one night, some intuition drove us to an area of grass on the edges of the Bois de Vincennes. It was a halfhearted lawn, bordered by a strip of concrete rather like a sidewalk, with sparse, dry grass. There was a bench there. We sat and started pressing up against each other, not really caring that the place was lit by a streetlight and quite a way from the edge of the forest. It could have been a scene from a film in the late forties, when the camera pans out and isolates the characters in a halo of light. When Bruno lifted up my dress and started energetically stroking my pussy, the trees were out of focus. Even though we weren't really aware how unwise this might turn out to be, we didn't talk, and we did try to shrink the space we occupied by making only brief movements and taking turns to attend to each other. While his fingers delved between my thighs, I stayed curled up against him with my legs folded up as tightly as the position of my arms would allow. I had kept my top on. When it was my turn to bend over the bulge in his jeans, he sat motionless with his head on the back of the bench, his body stiff as a board. I began a deliberate blow job, avoiding any changes of rhythm so as to prevent any sudden reactions. Suddenly, a second, powerful light came on in the distance, aimed toward us. For a moment we froze expectantly, unable to identify exactly what this light was or where it was coming from. One of Bruno's characteristic responses was to let himself be sucked off passively, as if against his will, sometimes even interrupting to then start the process up again without any warning by grabbing his prick and aiming it at my mouth, as if he almost would have preferred entering by force. That is what he did then, bringing my head down by pushing on the nape of my neck. My lips and hand resumed their regular movement. None of the things that this brutal illumination of our soldered forms implied actually happened. The light shone on the side of my face, and it was so bright that it dazzled me through my closed eyelids. I saw the fellatio through to its peaceful conclusion in the half-silence of our breathing and with the black and gold splashes of light dancing before my eyes. Then we went home, sharing an amused feeling of perplexity we barely discussed. Had we been in the headlights of a car? A police car or a voyeur? Had a faulty floodlight come back on by itself? I never found an explanation for that perfectly focused light.

Open Air

If I heard anyone say of me "Fucking for her is like breathing," I would agree more than willingly because the expression could be taken literally. My first sexual experience, and many others since, took place in circumstances that could lead one to believe oxygen has an aphrodisiac effect on me. My nudity feels more complete to me out in the open than in a closed room. When the surrounding temperature, whatever it may be, can be felt by an area of skin it doesn't normally reach, such as the small of the back, the body no longer presents an obstacle to the air, it is penetrated by it and is, therefore, more open, more receptive. When the atmosphere that embraces the vastness of the world adheres to the surface of my skin like myriad tiny suction cups, my vulva also feels as if it has been drawn out and dilates deliciously. If a gentle wind blows across its threshold, the feeling is amplified: the labia feel bigger than ever, gorged with the air brushing past them. I will speak later, and in more detail, about erogenous zones, but I can say now that even the gentlest attention to the oft ignored area linking the anal depression to the triangle where the labia meet—that underrated rut between the asshole and the opening of the cunt—is guaranteed to subjugate me; feeling the air against that part of my body is more intoxicating than high altitude. I like opening up my buttocks and my legs to the flow of air.

There must be a fairly general intrinsic link between the idea of moving in space, of traveling, and the idea of fucking, otherwise the widespread expression "getting off" would not have been invented. Taking into account all these factors, terraces, roadsides, stretches of open country and any space designed merely to be passed through, such as concourses and parking lots, all of these are places (or nonplaces as the anthropologist Marc Augé would describe the latter) where it feels good to me to follow their example and be open.

The first time I took off all my clothes in front of several pairs of eyes, I was in the middle of a garden surrounded by a mesh fence. You already know about this. I have also referred to that other garden, which was in a particularly interesting site overlooking the sea. The garden stretched out in front of the house, and even though we were in the Midi, there was very little shade. Right at the front, an area of paving served as a sun terrace. We fucked there endlessly even in the heat of the day. Anyone flying overhead would have been amused, as you can be from an airplane, by the juxtaposition of contrasting scenes. It is always funny seeing the frantic streams of traffic on the outskirts of the city you have just left, but also, in the same glance, seeing the emptiness of the surrounding countryside. It isn't just that there is an abrupt join between these two images, running along the seam of a highway, but that they represent two conflicting things whose ignorance of each other is almost hostile; the speeding cars drawn magnetically to the city center seem to look down on the solitary vehicle fleeing to the countryside.

Up above Saint-Jean-Cap-Ferrat you could have seen an agglomeration of human bodies a little way away from a big house—abandoned for enigmatic reasons—but very close to a road where the cars heading for the cape and those returning from it passed each other continuously. It would have been difficult to make out the boundary that produced the mutual indifference between this group of people and these cars. The low gray stone wall at the bottom of the garden threw little shadow, and it would not have been obvious from the air that the road was several feet below the level of the garden. That particular summer I had two acolytes: a lesbian girlfriend and one of those girls met by chance on an outing who, because we liked her, became part of the group for the vacation.

We didn't spend much time in the villa except to sleep and to prepare meals, and our assiduous sunbathing had turned the terrace end of the garden into one of those meeting places that all households elect even when they are not necessarily the most convenient. New visitors arrived every day. With some, although of course not all, a bit of sunbathing or an afternoon siesta would see some developments. It was a sort of casual summer activity, like going out for a spin in a boat. Judith, who preferred women, nevertheless accepted anyone of either sex who expressed desire, with slightly detached good humor. She was a big girl, with the sort of body that is thought beautiful because it is—as they say—all in proportion, fashioned by a pantograph that simply amplified the blueprint of a slim girl. Her breasts were not heavy but shaped like cones with nipples perfectly in the center. The other girl had big, drooping breasts above a waist you could encircle with two hands. As I lay on my back, shifting my head away from the shoulder obscuring my view, I could see her thin frame silhouetted against the sky, and the heavy teardrops of her breasts undulating in the wake of her movements. I thought that her body couldn't possibly contain what she must have buried into it as she sat astride a particularly well-endowed member of the group. She had an angelic disposition, and we were an amicable trio with a constant appetite and no arguing. There was another girl, who stood head and shoulders above all of us and who coiled herself up when she fucked as if trying to leave more room for the other, smaller body ramming her so zealously, and I remember that once she burst a string of pearls with the tension in her flushed neck. Nothing ever disturbed the unspooling of those compact segments of the afternoon, their rhythm slowed further by the humming of the traffic absorbed into the buzzing of insects, and even though the clattering of those pearls on the ground was barely discernible and this girl in her rapture didn't moan any louder than anyone else, I was surprised by such a transport of ecstasy. I started to think: "Can a woman really experience such overwhelming pleasure that her body undergoes this sort of external transformation?" I was free to watch the fixed grimaces on some men's faces or, on others, the distant, absent mask, as their bodies reached maximum tension, when (in, for example, the classic position) they arch their spine from the lower back right up to the necks, peeling away from their partner's body with the same robust uplift as the prow of a schooner over the sea. But I watched women much less, and without the mirror they could have held up to me, I had no image of my own body at such moments, even though I am not short on narcissistic tendencies. I knew how to take up the right position and what moves to make; beyond that, everything was diluted into sensations that I didn't connect with any visible manifestations. If I can put it like this, these feelings didn't take on a physical form, even less so in the suave pleasures of the open air. There were times when I liked to withdraw, to detach myself from the great human centipede writhing on the beach mattresses, and to lie down on the wall just as I was. The light was too bright to stare up at the sky. If I turned my head to one side, the horizon was on a level with my eyes; on the other side, I had to close them because the light bounced off the pale paving stones.

Now here is a position I really like: arching my back down to facilitate access to my pussy so that it can be decisively nailed from behind while contemplating a wide panorama. As Jacques has a predilection for impromptu fucks in the countryside, I'm not deprived of these opportunities. In the region where we vacation, lots of trails lead to dead ends in the vineyards. We come to one of these dead ends, high up and abandoned, and, avoiding the brambles, pick our way to the dry stone wall. Because I don't want to take off my sneakers, I stretch my panties wide as I remove them. I am wearing a shirtdress, which I have unbuttoned, and Jacques lifts it up over my back. With outstretched arms and clutching my rolled-up panties in one hand, I lean precariously against the crumbling stones. In these circumstances there are not always preliminaries; Jacques enters my pussy, which gradually opens up, squeezing the spare flesh under my waist firmly in his hands. With my head hanging down, I can look into the darkened room of my body as it bends over itself, my breasts hanging down and swinging, the regular undulations of my stomach and, at the end of the narrow gallery, where the light appears again, a little bit of the crumpled surface of his balls and, intermittently, the base of his member. Watching the very short, very measured coming and going heightens my excitement as much as if not more than the stroking itself.

I curve my back still further and lift my head to offer more resistance to Jacques's hips as they smack more sharply against my ass. On the slopes of the little hill we're overlooking, there are no more vines, only scrub. When my cunt has been sensitized to its very depths, I just have to close my eyelids, and through my eyelashes, I can see the village of Latour-de-France over to the right. I still have the faculty to think to myself: "There's Latour-de-France" and to appreciate not for the first time its picturesque position on an outcrop of rock in the middle of the valley. The landscape spreads wider before me. I recognize the moment when my pleasure won't go any further (when I've come, however intensely), and I let Jacques come; he paces his thrusts more slowly until the final three or four of orgasm, while my mind abandons itself to another fulfilling pleasure: floating freely, it hovers over and follows the contours of each hill, clearly distinguishing each from the next, and sinking into the inky magic of the mountains in the background. I so love this constantly changing landscape, revealed as a series of planes falling heavily in front of one another, and right there and then I am happy to be flooded and overflowing with come welling up in the depths of my belly.

Céret is a noble-looking town set in countryside that still has a wild quality. There are very good restaurants there. Having arrived late one afternoon, too early to sit down and eat straightaway, Jacques and I decide to climb up to a sandy track some four or five meters wide. It slopes gently, and the ground is level so I don't even have to take off the very high black patent-leather heels I'm wearing for the occasion. In the near dusk the contrast between the white path and the high dark vegetation bordering it is more striking. On the valley side, breaks in the foliage afford glimpses of the over-lapping expanses of rustic tiles, which contradict the perception you have of the town when you walk between its elegant eighteenth-century facades, along its avenues roofed by thirty-meter-high plane trees. You would think that the entire plain had been pushed by the sea like a vast barge, and had forced the town to huddle itself against the mountainside. We stop and, standing one in front of the other, pick out other villages as if looking at a map. More cautious men take you first by the shoulders and your breasts, tickling around the base of your neck with their lips. But Jacques always starts by taking hold of the buttocks. He immediately grasps the fact that there is nothing under my designer houndstooth-check, bustier dress, which I shed in one swift movement as if sloughing off a skin. He slips in from behind, gently exploring my pussy with his little probe, but not trying to penetrate. I press my back against him. The air temperature is perfect. A correlation develops between the space around us and the way his hands wander expansively over my breasts and stomach.

I do, however, avoid these caresses because, even when his dick has really stiffened, I don't take it in my cunt before devoting just the briefest fellatio to it. At last I offer my rump. Balancing on my heels, with my legs slightly bent to be at the right height for the lovely, lubricated tip, I put my hands on my tensed thighs and spread my fingers. It is quite a tiring position to maintain without any other support. But what a good hammering I got that evening, my rear end grasped between his hands, pinioned and kneaded, with my top half thrust forward over the Roussillon plain as it slowly dissolved! I can clearly remember then thinking to myself, in one of those hyperconscious states crystalized by pleasure, that one day I would have to find a way of putting into words the extreme sensation of joy when two bodies that are joined together feel as if they are unfurling. To understand this, you just have to imagine those time-lapse shots you see in shows about the wonders of nature that show the petals of a rose suffusing with oxygen and methodically smoothing themselves out.

We are all subject to social laws and under obligation to family rites: we conform to what is now called "business culture," and even in the intimacy of our sexual lives we instigate habits and institute a code applicable to only two people—a "couple culture," you could say. So al fresco sex forms part of Jacques's and my couple culture. In the same way that I have put colored thumbtacks into a globe to show the places I have visited, I could mark off on detailed maps the ruins and the rocks, the bends in the road and the clumps of trees where someone looking through binoculars could have stumbled across the quiverings of a minute two-headed silhouette. Early one morning, against the sour-milk-colored rocks of a steep mountainside, me with my body braced in its usual position, clutching the narrow trunk of a young tree with sparse foliage, with my shorts scarcely lifted. We are joined by a second man: are we in the area on vacation? Have we lost our way? Once he has moved away, we speculate that—to avoid possible burglaries—he must work guarding the hermitage, which was in fact the reason for our climb. Another chapel, this one in ruins but still with high walls standing proud on a flat plateau with a crisscross of little walls around it, those of the long crumbled sacristy where it's good to walk and imagine its inhabitants, as in an ancient ruin. The short nave is in full sunlight, the choir in the shade, the altar of dark gray stone is intact. I lie down on it, too high off the ground to be taken there. While Jacques leans over and amuses me with a few playful licks, I keep my eyes wide open, gazing at the sky defined by the ridge of black walls; I could be at the bottom of a well. Once again we end up upright, in a tiny space just big enough for the two of us, and whose use we can't really guess. A corridor? A recess for a long-lost statue?

Other ruins, other razed spaces, this time a huge fortified farm and its outbuildings, and the plateau that—from its steep banks—it still seems to defend. I should point out another particular of our couple culture: between a third and a half of our sexual embraces are an interlude in a photo shoot. On this occasion the latter was long and complicated. I've brought a variety of clothes, some very delicate, and I'm afraid of catching them in the bushes and the piles of stone. Same problem when I have to change clothes between poses, especially with a silk chiffon dress that corkscrews in the wind. Jacques is going for light contrast and gets me to explore every nook and cranny of the ruins. I walk carefully over the stony ground because my shoes have sharp, high heels and pointed toes that hurt. I also have to avoid the goat droppings because, before we turned this ruin into a photographic studio, a herd of goats used it for grazing. More than once, I climb the walls barefoot, then Jacques hands me the shoes and I slip them on for a few poses. For each pose, I have to find a compromise between the precise position Jacques asks for (down to the last centimeter of how much pubic hair is showing and how wide the thighs are spread, or how tightly the see-through top fits) and the pain in my feet as I try to balance or position my buttocks next to clumps of brambles. While my gaze wanders over the 360 degrees of the panorama, my body is reduced to an extremely narrow margin for movement. Once in position, I obey my instructor reluctantly. Then, before the film runs out, I in turn ask him to take a last few pictures of me walking naked along the wide path that slopes gently back down to the car, left in the middle of the plateau. After so many constraints, I need to move forward in the hot air like an animal of the savannah.

The open door of the four-by-four will be an unnecessary screen; we've already seen that there isn't a car anywhere near the sole inhabited house on the plateau, and its inhabitants must, therefore, be out. Is it because of the two hours spent within reach of thousands of nature's lowly little assaults, or perhaps because of my hovering suspicion that Jacques has recently grabbed other asses than mine behind this metal screen? My vagina isn't ready. In these instances, I separate the lips and moisten them hastily with saliva surreptitiously tranferred to my finger tips. There will still be a bit of resistance, but the glans will scarcely have forced its entry before the juices have started flowing and soon the whole cock will have assumed its place in a suitably moist cunt. I think that first I put one leg forward and pushed it against the running board, perhaps to open the vulva a little farther, but it must be said that, if I have to turn my back on my partner, I like nothing better than jerking my ass back against him. To do this I have to keep my waist limber and it's better to have my feet together. The more I stick my ass out toward him, the more I can fantasize that my ass has taken on the autonomy normally attributed to the head—the seat of thought which lives on independent from the rest of the body—thus, my ass is the counterpart of my head. While I sought out Jacques's organ as if I were going to yoke it up to myself, I caught a glimpse of myself in the rearview mirror, with my body connected to his and to the whole background. When I see myself in the act, my features seem devoid of expression. There must be moments when, like everybody else, I make faces, but when I chance across a reflection in a window or mirror, I don't look the way I think I do; at that moment my gaze is vague, looking inward as onto a open space, but trusting, as if trying to find some point of reference.

The practice of open-air fucking became anchored in the way Jacques and I organized our lives right from the beginning of our relationship. A visit to his grandmother in a nondescript little village in the Beauce region included a compulsory stop by the side of the road. He would park the 2CV on the shoulder, we would nip through a hedge and find a field rising gently up to the horizon, then we would disappear into the grass. We had to wriggle about laughably to get out of our tight-fitting jeans. I would put my jacket down on the grass under my head for fear of insects, and Jacques's jacket protected the small of my back. Having not grown up in the countryside, I took naive pleasure in these hasty couplings of just two half-bodies; suddenly my legs and buttocks were not at the same temperature as the upper half of my body, which was still clothed, and Jacques somehow had to manage with his underpants and the waist of his trousers hampering his thighs. There is a childish pleasure in those naked parts getting off, as if the swaddled other half were an alibi.

The Mediterranean landscape in which we took to living for several weeks a year is very rugged, but its low vines and scrubland offer hardly any hiding places and even fewer natural beds. There isn't any grass, and as there are no trees, I often had to hang on to the windowless door of an abandoned car or to the uprights at the opening to a pigsty, my rear end jutting out all the farther as my eyes and nose struggled with its stench.

We often used a track that led up to a field of young vines planted in crushed white rocks, a track that has almost disappeared since we stopped using it. We identified some favorite spots along that track as time went by. Halfway up, right before it steepened, it widened out onto a sandy platform, and all along one side the sand gave way to an outcrop of curved rocks; you could have fun imagining that they were the backs of hippopotamuses breaking through the muddy waters of a river that also bore along dented old gas cans and broken pallets. I could lie down on the smooth surface of the rocks with Jacques leaning on his arms like an awning above me, giving me a few quick thrusts of his cock. But it wasn't easy for him to get deep enough in this position. The solution was for me to turn around and get on all fours, like the Roman she-wolf on her pedestal, receiving the very special offering of her devoted priest.

Farther up there was a hairpin bend in the track. On one side, there was a ditch that acted as a dumping ground, and every time we passed, we noticed that its contents had mysteriously changed: the carcasses of agricultural machinery, the Cyclops heads of washing machines, etc. On the other side, a pale colored rock ran along it for several meters, shear like a wall. Despite the intensity of reflected light, it was one of our elected stopping points, because there, too, the smooth rocks comfortably accommodated the palms of my hands, but also—and why not?—because we unconsciously liked to feel that our bodies came from the jumbleness around us. As there were no leaves to wipe ourselves with, and we didn't always think to come equipped with handkerchiefs, I would stay turned toward my rock for a few moments, with my legs apart, watching the come falling from my pussy onto the ground in a lazy drool the same whitish color as the rocks. Farther up again, on top of the plateau, the track ended in a huddle of trees where the remains of picnics sometimes mingled with the dry bushes, which might have offered a bit more shade. But we stopped there only a few times. You had to get there in the first place, and when we did, the business had often already been seen to. Jacques would not have been able to resist the undulating buttocks under the skirt or shorts in front of him, their movement as regular as breathing, marking out the rhythm as I walked; while I would be making the ascent absorbed in the thought of his eyes on me, giving me plenty of time to ready my cunt, which I can compare only to a baby bird's tirelessly gaping beak.

For some indiscernible reason, then, the couple culture I am describing played out its adventures mainly in bucolic settings. It's true that fucking in sunken tracks is less risky than on the porches of buildings, though I'd hasten to point out that, with other lovers, both Jacques and I did use urban locations. But Métro station corridors (where an employee uses the jostle of the crowd to brush imperceptibly over my buttocks—a tacit invitation to join him in a storeroom cluttered with pails and brooms) and little cafés in the suburbs (where joyless men take me in turns on a bench seat in the back room) are places I have visited with Jacques only in my imagination. And even then, was I taking him there? I have stopped doing it now, but there was a time when I liked to redecorate the room with my elaborate fantasies, gradually detailing the settings and the positions I adopted, in an almost questioning tone of voice because I would wait for Jacques's acquiescence, which he would grant in a neutral voice and with the indifferent spontaneity of someone who's thinking about something else (but he was probably only feigning indifference), while his tool worked sweetly and steadily. I draw two conclusions from these points.

The first is that, within a couple, each person brings his or her own fantasies and desires, and these combine into shared habits that then modulate and adjust to one another and, depending on the extent to which each partner wants them to be realized, cross the barrier between dream and reality without losing any of their intensity. My obsession with numbers found its realization when I practiced group sex with Claude and with Éric, because that was how their desires fused with mine. On the other hand, I did not feel any frustration at never taking part in group sex with Jacques (even when he told me he had done so without me); it must simply be that that was not the way in which our shared sexuality expressed itself. It was enough for me to tell him about my adventures and to intuit that they found some resonance in his fantasies, just as it was enough for him that I was a willing accomplice for his photographic reportages in those variously polluted landscapes, and an exhibitionist ready to expose herself for his lens—even if my vanity would have preferred more flattering backgrounds and more stylized portraits . . .

The second conclusion is that natural spaces do not feed the same fantasies as urban spaces. Because the latter is by definition a social space, it is a territory in which we express a desire to transgress codes with our exhibitionist/voyeuristic impulses; it presupposes the presence of others, of fortuitous looks to penetrate the aura of intimacy that emanates from a partially naked body or from two bodies soldered together. Those same bodies out under the clouds, with only God as their witness, are looking for the opposite sensation: not to make others come into the pocket of air in which their rapid breathing mingles but, thanks to their Edenic isolation, to let their pleasure spread as far as the eye can see. The illusion there is that their ecstasy is on the same scale as this expanse, that the body housing them is dilating to infinity. Perhaps the tipping into unconsciousness known as the *petite mort* is felt more keenly when the bodies are in contact with the earth, teeming with invisible life and in which everything is buried.

Granted, most of my masturbatory fantasies take place in urban settings (apart from those already mentioned, the following is often called up: a man in a packed Métro train presses his fly up to my buttocks and manages to hitch up my clothes enough to slip his dick in; his maneuver is not lost on other men, who flow through the crowds to take his place; the carriage is divided between those taking pleasure and those taking offense, the factions start arguing—try and find a more Parisian fantasy!), and I managed to make do with the hard shoulders of main roads and with the parking lots of the capital. Even so, when all is said and done, I think I prefer vast open spaces.

Now at night, cities give the illusion of vastness. When Claude and I started living together, we would get home late to our little apartment in the suburbs, I would walk ahead of him and, without any warning, lift my skirt up over the naked globes of my ass, not as an invitation for him to fuck me there (I don't think we ever did), nor to shock a potential passerby, but to breathe in the road around me, to let its refreshing breeze reach my quivering crack. In fact, I wonder whether the men from the clumps of trees and the parking lots, by their sheer numbers and their shadowy nature, aren't made of the same substance as space, whether I didn't rub myself up against shreds of the same fabric as air though with a slightly closer weave. More specifically: I have an unrivaled ability to find my way on an unfamiliar road. Perhaps this aptitude for passing from one man to another within a group, or for navigating—as I did at certain times in my life—among a number of different relationships, perhaps it belongs to the same family of psychological predispositions as a sense of direction.

Different Towns, Different Men

Throughout the first few years of my adult life, my sexual experiences were intimately linked with the need for escape, for open air. That need even instigated them. It was when I ran away from home for the first time that I lost my virginity. I had argued with my parents yet again. Claude, whom I did not yet know, had rung at the door of our apartment to let me know that a mutual friend I was supposed to meet had been delayed. He asked me to go out with him. In the end, his Renault 4 took us all the way to Dieppe. We set up the tent on the edge of the beach.

Sometime later I fell in love with a student from Berlin. We did not make love together (he was a cautious young man, and I had not made any demands), but his long, sturdy frame lying next to mine and his big white hands sent me into ecstasies. I wanted to go and live in West Berlin. The wide Kudamm leading all the way up to the gleaming blue cathedral, and the parks of that great city—even though it was divided at the time—fueled my dreams. And then the student wrote and told me that it would not be sensible for us to be committed when we were so young. Another excuse to run away, again with Claude (whom I still saw) and his Renault 4. Destination Berlin, to talk with the boy who wanted to break up with me. An attempt to cross the border between East and West Germany which failed because I did not have the necessary papers. So the student came as far as the frontier to talk things out, and my first romance came to an end in a cafeteria on a huge parking lot in the middle of a forest, amid lines of people and lines of cars waiting to pass the wooden sentry boxes.

Unfortunately, I retained this propensity to flee without warning for many years, which was fair to neither the man I was living with at the time nor those who had brought me to my destination, nor those I had gone to meet and would abandon to return home. This restlessness was partly due to the febrile interest that we had (Claude, Henri, a few others and myself) in the New World of sex, an attitude that would sometimes make one of us strike out on our own. The unspoken law expected this pioneering scout to come back and tell of his or her adventures. Which, of course, was not always the case, hence the mixture of oil and water that constituted, on the one hand, our disparate desires and, on the other, our libertarian minds. Going away for two days with a man I barely knew, or, as I did for several years, carrying on a relationship with a colleague who lived in Milan, was just as worthwhile for the journey and the change of scenery as it was for the promise of being bedded, touched and fucked in a fresh and unfamiliar way. If it had been possible, I would have liked to wake up each morning to the shadows of an as yet unexplored ceiling and to climb out of the sheets and stay for a few moments in the no-man's-land of an apartment where I had forgotten overnight which corridor led to the bathroom. At times like that, it is the other body that you leave behind, a body you may have known only a few hours but which, during those hours, nourished you with its solid presence and its smell; it is that body which provides your only source of the ineffable well-being of the familiar. How many times have I thought, as I fantasized languidly about the life of high-class whores, that that was one of the advantages of their job. As for the journey itself, the time lapse we inhabit when we are no longer in one place but not yet in the next, it can be a source of pleasure measured on the same scale as the erotic. In a taxi, when all the bustle that precedes departure suddenly falls away, or descending into that semiconscious state while waiting at an airport, I can sometimes feel the unmistakable sensation of a giant hand inside my body, squeezing my entrails and drawing from them a sensuous delight that pervades my every extremity, exactly like when a man looks at me in a way that implies he has me in his sights.

In spite of this, I have never used the frequent long-distance journeys necessitated by my work to collect lovers. I fucked infinitely less when my timetable was more flexible than it is in Paris, and when I could have made the most of those casual relationships with no tomorrows. However hard I try to remember, I can think of only two men whom I have met on a journey and with whom I had some form of sexual contact during the journey itself. And when I say contact, there was only one instance each time, between breakfast and the first meeting of the morning with one, and during what was left of the night with the other.

There are two explanations. First, right at the beginning of my career, a more experienced female colleague had led me to understand that conferences, seminars and other meetings held in seclusion with people who were temporarily cut from their usual ties were God-given opportunities for furtive creepings up and down hotel corridors. I was used to sexual rendezvous of a more advanced nature; nevertheless, this shocked me to the same extent as the shapeless clothes people wear to show that they are on vacation, when they are usually very particular about their appearance. With the in-

transigence of the newly converted, I believed that fucking—
and by that I mean fucking frequently and willingly whoever
was (or were) the partner (or partners)—was a way of life. If
not, if this thing was permitted only when certain conditions
were met, at predetermined times, well then it was just a
vacation from values that remained completely traditional.
(A little aside to put this severe verdict into context. We no
longer need so much to prove that our sexual tendencies can
turn inside out like an old umbrella, and the device that protects us when the wind blows with reality can flip the other
way and leave us to get soaked in the squalls of our fantasies.
Once again, I am bringing together fact and fantasy, in this
case to expose an amusing antinomy: despite the moral stance
I have just expressed, I have often been aroused by imagining myself as a "scumbag" for a group of stressed executives
at a conference; each would shoot his load into me secretly,
hiding at the back of a hotel bar, even in a phone booth, with
the receiver in one hand while carrying on a ritual conversation with the wife: "Yes, darling, it's going well, but the food's
not so great," etc. That's a sure-fire scenario to get me off on
my own complete degradation.)

In the realms of reality, though, the exotic adventures of
this spelunker of Parisian parking lots can be dealt with in
just two paragraphs. The assistant who had so emphatically
drawn me to him right in the middle of the hotel foyer did
indeed come and wake me up the following morning. Judi-
ciously, he had let me rest after our long travels—we were
crossing Canada—over the last few days. He pushed his hips
calmly. I let him get on with it without much conviction, but
I encouraged him almost as a professional would, nonethe-

less choosing a vocabulary that was rather more amorous than obscene. Afterward he said, quite sincerely, that he had been thinking about it for several days, but that he had waited until the end of the trip so as not to disturb our work. We worked together a number of other times. He never made the slightest gesture of sexual invitation again, and neither did I. It was the first time a sexual exchange that had started with someone whom I was to see again did not continue, did not naturally fertilize the soil of our relationship as friends and colleagues. It has to be said that I was at a stage in my life where I was trying with limited success if not to be faithful, at least to limit myself. I thought that these might be the venal transgressions permitted to people who were not libertines. It was the only time in my life that I vaguely regretted a sexual act.

A Brazilian adventure left me with more complex feelings. I had just arrived in Rio de Janeiro for the first time, and of all the telephone numbers I had been given, the only person to reply was a certain artist. As luck would have it, he was familiar with an area of French cultural history that was my field, and we stayed up very late, chatting on a gloomy terrace in Ipanema. Several years went by, he came to Paris, I went back to Brazil a couple of times. In São Paulo, as we came away from a party for the Biennial, we took the same taxi. He gave the address of my hotel. Without taking my eyes off the back of the taxi driver's neck, I drummed my fingers lightly on his thigh. He gave the address of his hotel. The bed stood by a bay window, and street signs outside threw blocks of yellow light across it as in an Edward Hopper painting. He did not lie over me and cover me, he sowed parts of his body like gentle seeds over mine, reassuring himself that

I was there with his hands, his lips, his penis, as well as his forehead, his chin, his shoulders and legs. I felt good as I sank into the depths of a migraine, which terrified him. I could hear him whispering about the time, all that time. There was no second time with him, either. Later, in another taxi, in Paris this time, as I watched rather than listened to him speaking to me attentively, I was overcome by an intense feeling of joy: I was thinking about the geographical distance between us, the long intervals of time between our meetings, which were nevertheless regular—sometimes, when in Rio, I might give him a quick phone call; and I thought of that single occasion when time and space had come together and their union had formed a perfect architecture.

The other explanation for the limitations in my adventures while traveling is connected with a subject I raised in the first chapter. I liked to discover—on the condition that I had a guide. I liked it if a man was introduced to me by another man. I would take my cue from the relationship the one had with the other, rather than having to think about my own desires and how to satisfy them. In fact, feeling desire and having sex were almost two separate activities; I could want a man very much and feel no frustration if nothing ever actually happened. I was a dreamer, a gifted fabulist; a major part of my erotic life was lived like that, heightened by the friction on my vulva, held between my thumb and index finger. Sex really answered a wider necessity: to carve a smooth path for myself in the world. As I have illustrated, I was living in the comfort of a familial complicity; something you do not get when you arrive for the first time (and without any specific tips) in some distant city.

With many men, it is their houses that I remember before anything else. That is not an excuse to underestimate other memories that I have of them; it is rather that they cannot be dissociated from their background, and it is a spontaneous reconstruction of this background that brings back a moment of affectionate friendship or the geometry of bodies. The reader may well have realized: I quickly take in the setting. When my most intimate opening has given access, I have opened my eyes wide, too. I learned to use this method, among others, to find my way around Paris when I was very young. An architect friend whom I used to visit in his Parisian pied-à-terre on the top floor of a new building—so high up that the view from the bed dived straight into the sky—once commented that from my place in the rue Saint-Martin on the Rive Droite to his at the top of the rue Saint-Jacques on the Rive Gauche, you just had to follow a straight line. I came to love the area around Invalides when I accompanied my dentist friend on his trips to one of his girlfriends. She had been a successful variety singer in the 1950s, and she still had the bland and uptight appeal of record covers of the period. She submitted with lukewarm enthusiasm, and I amused myself by playing the aesthete, scorning the low tables cluttered with a collection of tortoises of all sizes, in stone and in porcelain, and going to gaze through the windows at the sublime proportions of the buildings along the esplanade.

Each home elicited a specific way of looking at it. In Éric's apartment, the bed was the nerve center in a kaleidoscopic arrangement of camera lenses, screens and mirrors; in Bruno's, based on the model of Mondrian's studio, a vase of flowers was the only focal point in a space where the doorjambs, the beams, the frames of the cupboards and the furniture all seemed to be one continuous unit, all with homogenous proportions, as if the same volume repeated several times served a variety of functions, as if the big dining table, for example, was merely an elevated replica of the bed.

I carry in me a sweet nostalgia for large apartments in Italian cities. When my collaboration with Enzo began, he was living in Rome, in what I think was an outlying part of the city, in one of those ocher-colored buildings separated from others by open spaces. When I compared this place to the suburb of my childhood, I was amazed that there was so much space lying fallow. There must have been a sort of feudal urbanism dictating that each building should be able to project its entire shadow on the ground in the evening. Inside, the rooms were much larger than those in French apartments of a comparable standard. One's voice echoed in the bathroom, and the title that covered the floor of the entire apartment was so clean that it made it all the easier to appreciate the full extent of the space, as if someone had just finished buffing it, in honor of our visit. After a couple of years, Enzo moved to Milan. The buildings were older, the apartments even more spacious, the ceilings higher. There was no more furniture. It was such a pleasure wandering around it with nothing on, as pristine as the fresh paint on the walls, as close to my essence as the bedroom was to its, furnished as it was with only a bed and an open suitcase! Pulling off my sweater and letting my skirt slip to the floor caused an inrush of air that aroused my entire body.

On the Threshold

The reader will understand more readily why I have made such an intimate connection between physical love and a mastering of space when I explain that I was born into a family of five living in a three-room apartment. And the first time I escaped the place was the first time that I fucked. That was not why I left, but that was what happened. Those who have been brought up in more well-off families where each member has his or her own room where privacy is at least respected, or also those who have walked to school in the country, may not have had the same experience. Discovering one's body would not have been so much of a tributary to the need to expand the space within which the body moved. Whereas I had to cover geographical distances to reach parts of myself. I had to go from Paris to Dieppe in a Renault 4 and to sleep facing the sea to learn that somewhere in a part of me I could not see and had not imagined, I had an opening, a cavity that was so supple and so deep that the extension of flesh that made a boy a boy, and me not one, could be accommodated there.

The expression has fallen into disuse, but it used to be said of a young boy or girl who was not supposed to know how the human race is perpetuated—and by extension how love and the satisfaction of the senses are connected—was "innocent." I remained almost completely innocent until I had direct experience of the first act of that process. I was twelve when my periods started. My mother and grandmother got into a state and called the doctor, my father popped his head around the door and asked with a laugh whether I had a nosebleed. So much for teaching me the facts of life. I had no clear idea of where this blood was coming from, and I couldn't distinguish between the passages through which my urine and my periods passed. One day the doctor tactfully explained to me that I should clean myself rather more thoroughly than I had been with my washcloth; otherwise, he said, sniffing the latex-covered finger that had examined me, "it doesn't smell very nice." I eventually suspected something because of a scandal at a rock concert. My mother and her friends were talking about it in front of me. The concert had caused an outbreak of violence, and the police had had to intervene. "Apparently some of the girls were so far gone that they even took the billy clubs and stuck them up themselves!" Put them up where? And why exactly would they want billy clubs? Questions that unsettled me for a long time.

I was an adolescent but had retained the ignorance of my infantile onanism. As a very young girl, I had realized that some games afforded me exquisite and incomparable sensations. I played with dolls in a specific and unusual way. I would gather the crotch of my panties into a thick strip and wedge it into the cleft between my legs right up to my buttocks, and I would sit down so that the fabric dug into me slightly. In that position, I would take the tiny concave hand of a plastic Ken doll and let it roam over a naked Barbie. In later years I replaced the action of the bunched panties with a rubbing of the two swollen lips at the front of the cleft. I had stopped playing with dolls, but I would picture myself in a situation similar to that of the Barbie, and I was entitled to the same diet of caresses. Perhaps because this activity gave me so much satisfaction, I didn't try to find out more about the ways in which a man and a woman can be together. But here is the point I wanted to make: while, in my mind, several different boys ran their hands over my body, in reality that body remained hunched, almost paralyzed, apart from the tiny to-ing and fro-ing of my hand clamped in my groin. My mother had not slept with my father for several years. He stayed in what had been their bedroom, and she moved into the second bedroom to share the double bed with me, while my brother slept in a single bed to one side. Even when you haven't been told anything, you instinctively know which activities should be kept hidden. What a paradox that I should have been forced to acquire such dexterity to give myself pleasure while barely moving or breathing, so that my mother, who brushed against me when she turned over, wouldn't feel me quivering! The fact that I had to rely more on mental pictures than on blatant physical caresses may well have developed my imagination. Despite my best efforts, it did happen: there were times when my mother shook me and called me a dirty little girl. When I went to Dieppe with Claude, I was no longer sleeping in the same bed as my mother, but even then—and for many years—I still masturbated in a tightly hunched ball. Finally, I could say that when I finally opened my body, I learned to uncurl it.

Space rarely opens up to us all at once. Even in the theater, when one more curtain needs to be raised, the process can be laborious, the heavy fabric rises slowly or, when the scene is still half hidden, the mechanism gets stuck and some occult resistance defers by a few seconds the spectator's mental involvement in the action. It is well known that we attach special importance to the transitions in our lives and the places they occurred. The sensual pleasure I feel in airport lounges is perhaps a distant echo of the act of emancipation I achieved when I accepted Claude's invitation to go with him, and stepped through the door with no knowledge of what the end of the journey would bring. But space is only ever an immeasurably large balloon with a hole. If you blow it up too fast, it will readily turn on you and deflate just as quickly.

I must have been thirteen or fourteen when I belatedly witnessed a "primal scene." As I walked along the hall, I saw my mother on the threshold of our front door with the friend who used to come and see her when my father was away. They were exchanging a slight kiss, but her eyes were closed and her back was arched. I took it badly. She took the fact that I took it badly badly.

Three or four years later I first saw Claude framed in the same doorway. It was June. It was late when we arrived in Dieppe, and found a place to camp. We couldn't see very well to put up the tent. At the time a lot of students took amphetamines to keep them awake so that they could study through the night before an exam. Claude must have taken some so as not to get tired on the journey, and he offered me one. Inside the tent, we didn't sleep. When he asked me quietly whether he could penetrate me, I was trembling. I couldn't really say if it was because of what was happening or because of the drug. In any event, I felt thoroughly unsure about my state. A few months earlier I had indulged in some heavy petting with a boy. He had put his erection onto my naked stomach and had come there. The next day I got my period. My knowledge of physiology was so hazy that I thought this blood meant I had been deflowered. Particularly as, after that, I waited a very long time for my next period (young girls' cycles are often irregular and can be disrupted by emotional upheavals), and I thought that I was pregnant! I told Claude that I would say yes if he asked me the question again and used my name. He couldn't have been expecting that sort of demand, and he willingly said "Catherine" several times. When he withdrew, I was scarcely aware of a fine thread of brown along the top of my thigh.

The next day we hardly left the tent, where there was just room for our two bodies. We lay on top of each other and rolled over, separated from the people next to us by the canvas, through which a golden, sandy light filtered. There was a family in a nearby tent. I heard the wife asking irritably: "But what the hell are they up to in there? Aren't they ever going to come out?" and the man calmly replying: "Leave it! They're tired. They're resting." We did manage to extract ourselves from our lair to eat something on a little terrace. I was in quite a daze. As we headed back to the tent, I noticed that the beach and the campsite, which was set slightly back, were cut right across by a cliff that ran perpendicular to the sea.

I don't remember exactly how my parents got me back, but it was not without drama and not for long. A few weeks later there was the episode in the garden near Lyon. A few weeks after that, I went to live with Claude. The trip to Dieppe had allowed me to "become a woman," and I had established the right to come and go as I pleased. All the same, as I look back on it, our frolicking in the tent seems like child's play and reminds me of the way I used to hide from adults by pulling my sheet up over my head, creating the confined but vital space of a little house of my own. Succumbing to a forbidden activity in a place regulated by communal laws, poorly protected by a thin or flawed screen, by a bit of foliage, even by a wall of human accomplices, derives—at least in part—from the same ludic spirit. It represents an elementary mechanism of transgression that, paradoxically, belongs less to extroversion than to introversion; you don't make an exhibition of yourself, you turn in on your intimate pleasure, pretending to ignore the fact that it might accidentally erupt in front of spectators who are not expecting it and might even try to stop it.

3. Confined Space

A Variety of Havens

My explorations of exclusive locations on the outskirts of Paris not only filled me with the euphoria of wide-open spaces but, on the flip side, with that of a game of hide-and-seek. On a fairly broad street a stone's throw from the Soviet embassy, I once found my refuge in the back of a Ville de Paris van, because one of our group was a city employee. The men came in one by one. I knelt to suck them or lay down and curled to one side, the better to present my ass to facilitate their access. Nothing had been provided in the back of the van to soften the ridged surface of the metal floor, and each jolt was quite painful. But I could have hid there all night, not so much stiffened because of my uncomfortable position but rather dulled and lulled by the atmosphere of my unlikely haven where I curled up and sunk and like in those opaque dreams, watched myself sink deeper. I didn't have to move: the rear door was raised at regular intervals, the man jumped out and a new silhouette slipped in. In that creaky vehicle I was like a motionless idol unblinkingly accepting the homage of faithful followers. I was as I had imagined myself in some of my fantasies (like, for example, the one when I'm in a caretaker's quarters with only my ass protruding from the curtain, which serves to hide the bed), offered to a long succession of men who stood outside stamping their feet and yelling abuse at each other. A 2CV van is worth a caretaker's lodge any day. But I left my metal palanquin before they were all done. Éric, who had been keeping watch, explained the following day: on the one hand, the men were in such a state of excitement that they were beginning to get aggressive, and on the other hand, the van was threatening to tip over.

The cabs of semis are much better suited, mainly because they are equipped with a bunk. I can never catch sight of the girls waiting by the side of the road, their bodies covered in a patchwork of skimpy accessories, a demi bra glinting above the low-cut top—which doesn't quite meet the miniskirt, which allows a glimpse of the garter belt below—I can never see them without thinking of the little jump they have to make on one foot to reach for the step in order to get up to the customer. I am familiar with the impulsion the body needs and the brief subsequent ascension that carries that body up to two tough men who greet it delicately, accustomed as they are to limit their movements in the cramped cab. My good fortune was not having to name a price or to wait out in the cold. I didn't spend much on my outfit, either. I would wear just a coat or a raincoat that fell open like a dressing gown on the way up. Once when I was snuggled into one of these bunks—which just happened to be in an International Art Transport (one of the main transporters of art) truck parked near the Porte d'Auteuil—I received the most careful handling. On that occasion only one of the two truck drivers took care of me, at great length, to the extent that—to my surprise—he kissed me on the mouth and went on fondling me after he had come. The other one watched, first by adjusting the rearview mirror, and then he turned sideways but did not touch me. It got late, we chatted; it was a very convivial situation.

Snuggling down into a narrow bunk is an experience closely identified with childhood. Jacques and I shared one in a second-class sleeping car on the way home from Venice during a railworkers' strike, and we were trapped in a compartment with a big family. We had to come to some sort of arrangement. We had elected to have one bunk for the two of us, one of the very top ones, which are very hot and can't be reached without undertaking the most perilous and ridiculous contortions. The parents had taken the two bottom bunks, and the children had distributed themselves as best they could among the three remaining. We then settled into one of those lazy positions in which the human race will continue to derive certain delight for a long time yet (even if that means forgetting the entire repertoire of the *Kama Sutra*): that is, our bodies lay closely curled in a concave arc, and I warmed my buttocks against Jacques's lap. When all the night-lights had been switched off, we took our pants down and had a deep, slow fuck. Without a word or so much as a moan disguised as a comfortable sigh, with no movement other than the imperceptible contraction of Jacques's buttocks, which scarcely rolled his hips. Anyone who has been constrained to seize their pleasure in public involuntarily (in a boarding school dormitory, a small family home) knows what I am talking about: if you achieve your pleasure, then it will have absorbed the utter silence and the near paralysis of the bodies that were its preconditions, and it will have been the more intense for them. Understandably, people then try to re-create this lack of privacy in more or less artificial ways, and some try to achieve it by choosing the most unexpected and public nooks and crannies.

Listening closely to the breathing around us, which suspended its various regular rhythms when the train jolted sharply, I actually felt afraid on that bunk, me who would have been perfectly indifferent to, for example, hitch up my skirt on the platform if Jacques had had the urge to ask me—I was afraid that the children would guess what we were doing. It was as if I were sharing a bed with my mother, but I had changed roles; yes, I was still the one succumbing to clandestine activities, but I had become the adult who might feel disgust at the child's reaction. In fact, I had not forgotten the sense of decency that I'd had then, one that was all the more intransigent at that young age than one might think or appreciate precisely because it reflects the superiority of childhood to adulthood. Put differently, I may not have minded what the adults thought of me, but I did mind what the children thought. I didn't want to put before them something—not that they should not yet know—that was too serious and precious to reveal carelessly. Because I had relationships with men who had children, I twice very nearly gave them a far more graphic scene than my mother's sneaked kiss with her friend. The first time I spent the night with Robert in his home—in fact, the only time—I watched him wedge the door handle with the back of a chair. "Funny, those things you see in old action films really work!" I thought. In the morning, his daughter rattled the door, demanding to see her father before leaving for school. He yelled at her to go and get ready, and said he would come and see her. Which he did. On vacation once, during siesta time, Éric's son called his father from the other side of the cotton curtain that partitioned off the bedroom. Éric detached himself from my breast by leaning on an elbow, like the lid of box pivoting on a hinge. "Go away," he bellowed angrily. "Go on, get out of here and let me sleep!" Both times I felt for the rebuffed child.

...

When you pass a very large vehicle on a motorbike, however little wind there is, there is always a precise moment when the air snatches you. This moment comes when you have reached the front of the truck, just before you start to pull back into the lane. There is an in-draft, and your torso undergoes a double twisting motion. One shoulder is thrust forward, the other backward, and this movement is reversed just as sharply. You are like a sail snapping in the wind. Just seconds earlier you were cleaving through the space as it opened up before you. Suddenly, that space closes in and shakes you up, assaults you. I like this feeling and can identify it in various different situations: feeling that you are right at the heart of a space that opens and closes, stretches and contracts. And in that space you are like a rubber band that has been stretched and then released, and comes back to smack the hand holding it; you are alternately the subject that possesses its environment (even if only by looking at it) and the object possessed.

I felt this, quite unexpectedly, in a sexshop. I liked going there with Éric. While he kept the assistant busy with his requests, which were always extremely precise because he knew exactly what had just come out, especially video, I would wander around the shop. The first picture I saw, whatever it might be (a girl holding her scarlet vulva open with her manicured fingers, her head in the background, slightly raised, her gaze floating above her body with the same lost expression as a patient trying to see her feet at the end of a stretcher; another one sitting back on her heels in the traditional pinup pose holding her massive breasts in her open palms; a young man in a three-piece suit pointing his dick toward an older woman bending over her desk—she is a lawyer or CEO—and even bodybuilders intended for the gay clientele, strapped into G-strings that look minute in comparison to their bodies), any sort of picture, graphic, photographic, cinematic, be it realist or caricature (a model posing in the underwear pages of a mail-order catalog; great droplets of come splattered outside the margins of a cartoon), every image I would say even at first glance made me feel that characteristic nerve tingling deep between my thighs. I leafed through the magazines on display, cautiously turned over the shrink-wrapped ones. Isn't it wonderful how you can be aroused so freely, in full sight and full knowledge of all the other customers doing the same thing, even though each behaves as if he or she is searching through the display racks at the local newsstand? Isn't it admirable, the apparent detachment you have in public, contemplating pictures and objects that would certainly make you lose your composure at home? I liked to imagine myself in a mythical world where every shop offered that sort of merchandise, in among other goods, and where, with apparent nonchalance, you were gradually suffused by that warm feeling, absorbed in your perusal of organs reproduced in full color that perfectly depicted their moist surfaces, and you might shamelessly turn and show them to the person next to you. "Excuse me, could I borrow your paper?" "Oh, please do." Etc. The quiet, unassuming blatancy that reigns in a sex shop spread to every aspect of social life.

Going through into the back room where the peep show is going on is like arriving late at the theater. You are plunged into darkness, in a circular corridor lined with booths. You need coins, not to tip any ushers but to pay to illuminate the two-way mirror that looks out on the central stage where a girl or a couple undergo a series of unbelievably slow contortions. It is so dark in the little kiosk that I have never been able to see a thing around me, not even the walls, which amounts to being in a void. There is, though, a faint bluish light coming from the stage, and a beam of this light settles on the base of the member that I have just taken in my mouth, so that the perceptible space around me is reduced to this section of wrinkled flesh dotted with hairs, which I swallow rhythmically. Perhaps Éric has to go to the register to change a bill for some more coins. Having turned toward the window, I then don't recognize the hands that start smoothing over my exposed buttocks; I can believe that both the hands and indeed the buttocks are far, far away from me, also on the other side of the screen. Just after we go into the kiosk, we feel each other blindly, our eyes focused on the show, which we are discussing. We agree that the girl has a nice pussy. The guy is a bit too cutesy. Éric would really like to watch the girl and me bring each other off. I ask whether we could meet up with her afterward, etc. Then we are taken up in the acceleration of our own movement; the couple in the blue light becomes less real; they are merely the distant, almost subconscious projection of the images conjured in the minds of those busying themselves in the dark. The shadow bent over my back lets out a hoarse "Ahhh" as it smacks more firmly against my ass.

The fantasy exchange between the show and the real action, when you fuck while watching a peep show, is not as fluid as what happens when you watch a movie on television, occasionally releasing your own grip to follow the action on the screen, and using it as a pretext for changing position. While the flickering pixels blur boundaries so that the space they delineate becomes almost an extension of the space you are in, the window at a peep show is a hiatus that substantiates the separation between two symmetrical parts, one that can be crossed but remains tangible. Two further points: pornographic films have a story line that, however formulaic, holds your attention, whereas the action in a peep show evolves very little; finally, you can watch a film continuously or spend the night in front of the television, but the bottomless kiosk has a limit, which is attained when the timer runs out.

...

Who doesn't have, somewhere among their memories, some of those voracious kisses, those exchanges of tongues that suddenly made full use of their complement of muscles, their great length and their monstrous adhesion, exploring each other as well as the relief of their partner's entire mouth and lips? And didn't this obscene deployment happen on some doorstep, at the foot of the stairs in an apartment building or on the corner of a porch, just where the light switches are (but, of course, you hadn't used those)? Adolescents rarely have somewhere they can call their own, so their carnal displays take place in these semipublic spaces such as side doors, stairwells and landings. I have referred to the need—felt most keenly by the urban pubescent population—to establish an intimate sphere within forbidden spaces. The sexual instinct, which civilization has made secret, finds its first spontaneous expression not behind a closed bedroom door but in places we pass through, which belong to everyone and where courtesy reaches its peak of reserve: "Good morning. Good evening. I'm so sorry. After you," etc. The number of times I have had a breast mauled by clumsy hands in the exact spot where my neighbor usually holds the door for me. Even once I had become an emancipated adult, I still sometimes displayed sufficient masochistic impatience to let myself be manhandled like a heavy bag in a tiled hallway lit by the streetlights filtering through a vent, while I sat on the radiator with my knees under my chin and the cast-iron ridges digging a little farther into my buttock flesh with every slam. As a result, shouldn't we be asking ourselves whether the taste for transgression that encourages adults to choose this sort of place— and other, even more public and uncomfortable ones—to undertake the sexual act, whether this derives from some so-called primary transgression, and whether their "perversity" should not be put down to a venial immaturity?

Before I came to know the games played on the paths in the Bois de Boulogne or the exploits at the Porte Dauphine, my outings with Henri and with Claude allowed me to continue having these surreptitious petting sessions (pretty heavy, some of them) in the common space of Parisian apartment blocks. At the witching hour, when thieves are abroad, we disappeared into a group of buildings, looking for a friend's apartment. Even though she was an artist and always liked to appear very relaxed, rebellious even, she was bourgeois—we're talking the boulevard Exelmans here, quite a chic address—and on top of that, she was the girlfriend of the man who was our boss, Henri's and mine. Our aim is childish. We want to go and ring the doorbell and beg her most sweetly to forgive us for disturbing her. The ulterior motive is that at least one of the boys will succeed in ramming his persistent prick into the depths of her little cushion of moist flesh, impregnated with the smell of sleep. But we still have to know exactly which building and on which floor the girl was sleeping. Claude, very sure of himself, volunteers to explore one of the buildings floor by floor, probably deliberately leaving Henri and me to linger in another, where our search proves fruitless.

Henri is always tender in his movements; his fingers always seem slightly awkward, as if he uses them more to establish things than to hold them. I am usually more forthright. Standing clamped together, we start by stroking each other's buttocks. Mine are bare under my skirt. There is not much more of him than there is of me, and I like to take a man's ass in my hands and to be able to put my arms around him easily. I have been with tall, well-built men, but I have never snubbed the seductions of small men. If a man's size is comparable to my own, and I feel an equal division of physical strength in our embraces, I experience a very particular kind of pleasure, which probably includes the desire to feminize the man in question, or even a narcissistic illusion: by holding him I can experience the same pleasure he has in holding me.

I hope, later in the book, to do justice to the intoxication that overruns me when my mouth is filled by a stiff penis: one of the roots of this feeling is an identification of my pleasure with the man's; the more he arches his body, the more emphatically he moans, gasps or whispers encouragement, the more I feel he is expressing the frantic calling coming from deep within my own genitals. For now I must concentrate on describing the scene with Henri, given that I sucked him with what he called astonishing ardor. How did I go about it? Following the instinctual pressure of his pubis against mine, did I let myself fall at his feet, guided down the length of his body by the persistent embrace of my arms, and then, kneeling before him, did I, as I usually did, rub my face, cheeks, forehead and chin over a shape that by its form and hardness always remind me of a darning egg? The light went out. Henri joined me on the threadbare mat and we curled up together at the bottom of the stairs, facing the elevator shaft. I extricated the object that was imprisoned behind the straining fly and helped it assume the correct shape with slow, regular hand movements. Then, my head bent between his legs, I continued the motion with a similar to-ing and fro-ing of my mouth. The light came back on, suspending my progress. I felt the hammering of fear beating in my chest and ringing in my ears, its echoes reverberating as far as the erogeneous zones in my mound . . . But no sound followed the light. While we waited, I automatically kept my hand over his organ, which was now too swollen to be put back where it belonged. Then, reassured, we settled more comfortably on the stairs. Some of the rules of fucking, especially if it is performed in a place that does not lend itself to excesses, are like the rules of courtesy: the partners take turns devoting themselves to the other's body, temporarily keeping their own body out of reach, just like two people exchanging thanks or desultory compliments in a one-upmanship of unselfish attention. Henri's fingers triggered a spasm in my cunt like the connecting rod of a train, while I sat against the front of the stairs, taking only the surrounding light into my mouth and, although I still held his member in my hand, no longer rubbing it up and down. Then I considered myself sated for now, and it was my turn to close my thighs and bury my head back between his. Our movements took up no more space than our tightly joined bodies. The light went back on two or three times. In the intervals between, it was as if the darkness were hiding us in a crevice in the walls of the well formed by the elevator shaft. The blaze of light whipped my forehead to make me suck more quickly. I now don't remember whether Henri ejaculated by "day" or by "night."

The usual little patting movements with the flat of the hand to straighten out clothes and tidy hair. When Claude and I spent an evening with friends and I unexpectedly had a fuck—as I had that night—out of his sight, I couldn't meet up with him again without feeling slightly awkward. I think it was probably the same for whoever was with me. That night Claude was waiting for Henri and me at the foot of the stairs;

he pretended he had just come from another building. Henri thought he was behaving strangely. We gave up on the idea of finding the girl's door.

Sick and Dirty

Every confined place in which the body has felt a fulfillment inversely proportional to the available space, where it has felt all the more pleasure for being constrained, awakens in us a nostalgia for the fetal state. And we never benefit from it so much as when, safe in that secret haven, organic life reassumes its rights (whatever they may be) and we can abandon ourselves to something not unlike the beginning of a regression. If you think about it, it was not for reasons of hygiene that bathrooms became places in which we isolate ourselves, closets in fact. Modesty is the pretext given, but the occult explanation for this modesty is neither a fear for our dignity nor a wish not to embarrass others but the freedom to experience the pleasures of defecation without any restraint, to inhale our own permeating stench or even examine our stools meticulously, taking a cue from Salvador Dalí, who left descriptions rich with comparisons and images. I am not about to tell a series of scatological stories, I just want to remember here some banal situations in which my different bodily needs found themselves in conflict. And as I have never come across any declared enthusiasts for my farts or feces, and I myself have had no inclination to savor those of others, these confrontations turned out to be dubious struggles between pleasure and displeasure, ecstasy and pain.

I suffer from migraines. Having landed in Casablanca, I suffocate in the heat at the airport as I wait for ages for my luggage to come through. The journey is not over yet: Basile, the architect friend who invited me, drives me to the resort town he built, where he has a small house. We stop off on a track away from the road. It is the most beautiful day, the sparse leaves flitter in the bright light around us. Squatting on all fours on the backseat of the car, I am, as usual, sticking my ass out so far that I can almost imagine it as a balloon popping out of the car, ready to detach itself from the rest of my body and fly away. While this balloon is being pierced by one of the sharpest pricks I have ever known, I can feel the first symptoms. My vision is blurred by a sort of flashing that accentuates the fluttering effect of the light. By the final charge, my body—with the exception of my ass—has ceased to exist, emptied of its substance like a piece of fruit left to shrivel, crumbling in the glimmering light. Or, to be more precise, there is nothing left between my head, which has been turned to stone by the viselike grip of pain, and the skin on my buttocks, where the last few caresses linger. I could no longer utter a single word. When we arrived at our destination, I went and lay flat out on the deep, tall bed. Added to these two terminals to which my body was reduced (the one overwhelmed by pain, the other abandoned to lethargy by pleasure) was now the weight of nausea, which comes with very bad headaches. Now I had just the outward appearance of a body, anchored in three places by the only three organs left to me, and fussed over silently by an anxious man. When a migraine pins me in the depths of a darkened room like this, when I don't even have the strength to peel off the sheet impregnated with up to thirty-six hours' worth of old sweat, and when breathing the dissipated stench of my own vomit is the only perception left to me that does not cause intolerable pain, my last mental resources can end up imagining strangers watching me in that state (with the cavities around my eyes enlarged by rings of gray and the angle between the inner edge of my eyelids and the bridge of the nose pinched tightly together). Jacques is too accustomed to it, and doctors have too much clinical distance. I would like Jacques to take photographs of me at times like that, and for them to be published and seen by people who read my books and articles, for example. There would be some sense of compensation in closing the circle on my physical degeneration by inscribing it on the gaze of others.

My relationship with Basile has always been light and playful, and the pleasure unadulterated. If I had to be ill in front of him, then I would have to do it with the same simplicity with which I surrendered myself when he took me from behind after a good meal and I let my bulging tummy express a few farts. He was a sharp, astute man, and conversation with him was always stimulating, and one day he was kind enough to compliment me on the big nose that I had always had a complex about, but which he told me gave my face character. He was also someone who usually came in my ass, but not before having used a firm index finger to stimulate the most highly reactive point on my body. While I was no longer capable of exchanging a single word with him, or to respond to the touch of his hand, I could still offer him the spectacle of myself indulging in the complete negation of my being.

It is often extremely difficult to identify the cause of a headache; anyone who is prone to them will know this, and in some ways this spares them of any feelings of guilt when the cause is obvious and it is their fault: abuse of alcohol or too much sun. I haven't been drunk more than two or three times in my life. On one of these occasions I was with Lucien, who had slumped on top of me on the sitting room carpet, in front of his friends and unbeknownst to his wife. He had taken me for dinner with a young couple who lived outside Paris. I drank too much champagne without realizing it. The couple lived in a big bungalow where you walked straight into the kitchen, which also served as a dining room. At the back of the room there were two doors next to each other, each leading to a bedroom. The evening must initially have started in their bedroom. I am trying to piece it together: Lucien takes me over onto the bed with help from the other man; they start touching me up, I concentrate on investigating their flies. The young woman hangs back a bit; her boyfriend takes her by the shoulders, kisses her, encourages her to come and lie down with us. She goes into the bathroom, he follows her and comes back explaining that "this isn't Christine's thing, but we can do what we like, it doesn't bother her." I partake in the goings on in the same way that I involuntarily follow a radio play echoing through the courtyard of my apartment building on a summer's day when my neighbor's windows are open. Probably out of respect for Christine, even though she doesn't reappear—is she busying herself in front of the bathroom mirror or sitting indecisively on the side of the bath?—we move to the other bedroom.

I really can't remember whether our host penetrated me. On the other hand, I do know that I apathetically let Lucien have me. The eiderdown was a deep chasm, and I sank deeper into it. My vagina, worked over smoothly by Lucien (who must have realized I wasn't feeling well), softened and sank, drawn into that great depth, while a paralyzing force kept my head, neck, shoulders and even my partially spread arms flat on the bed. I did somehow find the strength to get up. How many times in the night? Four, five times? I crossed the kitchen naked and went into the garden. It was pouring with rain. I stood and vomited straight onto the ground in the middle of the alley, not even looking for somewhere to hide. It has to be said that each spasm converted the blacksmiths hammering inside my skull into something that felt like a final disintegration of the beaten piece of metal. The whole body flows into the mass of the head and forms a fist tightly grasping a lacerating blade. The cold rain momentarily appeased the pain. On my way back to the bedroom, I rinsed my mouth out in the kitchen sink. The following morning, when the lifesaving medicine had been brought from the drugstore and when it was all over, Lucien assured me that he had fucked me several times during the night and that I had seemed to enjoy it. It is one of the rare times when I was not conscious of what I was doing. A few months later the young woman came to see me. She and her boyfriend had had a terrible car crash. He had died, and his family had turned her out of the house they had lived in together. I felt genuine compassion for her while at the same time having a strange feeling that this was just the continuation of a nightmare.

Putting all these episodes together reminds me of another. Not after a very good meal, as with Basile; it was on a day when, to the contrary, I might have eaten something that wasn't very fresh, and I had an upset stomach. Lucien absolutely insisted on taking me from behind. However hard I tried to avoid this and to distract him with fervent fellatio, I couldn't stop him from delving his fingers right up close to the part of me that was sick, and I realized to my shame that they brought out a small amount of liquid matter. He buried his dick in there. The pleasure that this particular use of the rectum gives is obviously in the same family as that experienced in the seconds before the expulsion of fecal matter, but in this case the conjunction of the two was so narrow that it bordered on torture. I have never taken part in scatological games, either of my own free will or encouraged by a man with that sort of experience. I have noticed that when this sort of incident occurred at all, it was with men much older than I, both of whom could be deemed—although both for different reasons—father figures. When he withdrew, Lucien went to wash himself with no commentary other than to say I had been silly to make such a fuss because it had been so good. I felt I could trust him.

There is such a perfect feeling of well-being when you have, so to speak, left your body behind in excesses of pleasure with someone else, but you can recognize some aspects of that well-being when you leave your body behind in the opposite circumstances, in abjection or even the most intense pain. I have dealt with the theme of the open space we appropriate for ourselves, and of our temptation to let strangers look on our nudity like at a shopwindow. In these instances, we actually wear our nudity like a garment, and displaying it relates to the excitement we feel when, conversely, we prepare our bodies, dress them and put on our makeup, to seduce. I emphasize the word "excitement," the rising tide of desire waiting for a response from the outside world. It surely cannot be excitement that we feel when we recoil into the closed world of pain or in the immediate satisfaction of elementary functions: when the body doesn't have the strength to occupy any other space than the sunken outline carved into a mattress, when the spew of vomit splatters the feet, when a dribble of shit trickles between our thighs. If there is any pleasure in this, it is not that the body feels struck by something greater than itself, it is that it feels bottomless, as if by exteriorizing the activities of our entrails, we could accede to our entire surroundings.

If one of the meanings of the word "space" is emptiness—if when it is used without any qualification, it principally evokes a clear sky or a desert—a *confined* space is seen almost as automatically as a filled space. When I feel the need to return my aspirations to vast horizons, I happily transport myself on my imagination to a garbage area, usually the one at the foot of the building in which I grew up. Back to the wall between the corrugated surfaces of the cans, with a man who sets down his bucket of trash for the occasion. I have never enacted this fantasy, but I assiduously maintained a relationship with a man who lived in such a shambles and so much filth that this archetypal garbage area must have had a place somewhere in his unconscious. This same man was an aesthete, a clear and self-possessed theoretician with a rather precious way of speaking. His apartment consisted of two minute rooms whose walls were completely covered in shelves laden with books and records, distributed at random, and some of the shelves had given way under their weight. Three quarters of one of the rooms was taken up with the bed, where the top sheet and the blanket were always scuffed up in a heap, and which you could get into only after pushing aside books, papers and newspapers. In the second room it was not just the desk that looked as if it had suffered the vengeance of a burglar furious not to have found what he was looking for, but also the floor; it was covered with a maze of crumbling piles of books and catalogs, heaps of opened envelopes and crumpled paper, fanned-out sheaves of paper that one might think were still of some use. This, along with the dust, would have been nothing if it hadn't been for the glasses with the dried brown ellipses of long forgotten drinks in their depths, used as paperweights if they hadn't left their slimy circular imprint on other pieces of paper, if a grayish T-shirt or a stiffened face towel hadn't been jumbled into the bed sheets, if—when you wanted to locate a bar of soap in the sink—you didn't have to search through archaeological layers of cups and saucers encrusted with crumbs, like the mud still attached to recently exhumed relics. . . all of that made you heave.

I spent many nights in this hovel. The occupant seemed not to notice. The fact that he never accomplished that elementary act of comfort—brushing his teeth—was perpetually unfathomable. When he laughed, his upper lip raised the curtain on a yellow plaster dotted with black patches. As I was sure that all mothers taught their children this hygienic routine, I wondered exactly what level of amnesia he had achieved on the subject of his childhood. He liked to be finger-fucked up his ass. From the outset he would put himself on all fours, presenting his large rather white bottom, and his face serious while he waited. Then I would kneel squarely beside him with my left hand resting gently on his back or his hip, and my moistened right hand would start by rubbing round the outside of his anus, then I would put in two fingers, three, four. With my back bent and my frenetic arm movements, I must have looked very like a housewife desperately trying to stop a sauce from curdling, or someone proudly finishing up a home improvement. His moans had the same nasal resonance as his laugh. Measuring the fruits of my sustained efforts by listening to them afforded me such an extreme state of excitement that it was only with great regret that I abandoned the movement, which had become painful. Then we undertook a series of positions with the logic of acrobats who end up exchanging places as they flow from one movement to the next. I would substitute my tongue for my fingers, then I would slide underneath him to form the sixty-nine position, then it would be my turn to go on all fours. The acute level of pleasure that I then reached was also a recurring subject for interrogation.

Not many people knew his lair, and wallowing in it undoubtedly revived the childish predilection for sewers. Sewers are hidden places, not so much because it would be humiliating to be seen there but because, following the example of animals that release a powerful stench to put off a predator, we hide ourselves in them like a protective envelope, we take refuge in them like a nest that is all the more secure for being partly strewn with our own excretions. Even so, my friends were in a position to confirm that the man in question was dirtier than is usually acceptable for intellectuals who often neglect their physical appearance. I didn't discourage their questions or their comments. There was a controlled defiance in my response: "Well, yes, I go just as I am now—freshly showered and in clean panties—and rub myself up against that filth." Or, if need be: "I rub myself against him just like I'm cuddling up to you."

You don't have to be a great psychologist to deduce from this behavior an inclination for self-abasement, mixed with the perverse intention of dragging others into that same abasement. But this tendency doesn't stop there; I was carried by the conviction that I rejoiced in extraordinary freedom. To fuck above and beyond any sense of disgust was not just a way of lowering yourself, it was, in a diametrically opposite move, to raise yourself above all prejudice. There are those who break taboos as powerful as incest. I settled for not having to choose my partners, however many of them there may have been (given the conditions under which I gave myself, if my father had happened to be one of the number, I would not have recognized him), and I can also say whatever sex there may have been and whatever their physical and moral qualities may have been (in the same way that I have never tried to avoid a man who didn't wash, I have with full knowledge had sexual contact with three or four who were completely spineless and stupid). And I was still waiting to find myself under a trained dog, as Éric kept promising, but which never happened, either because the opportunity just didn't arise or because he thought it ought to stay in the realms of fantasy.

Earlier on in this book, I applied my thoughts to the theme of space. I have now just spoken of animals and of immersing oneself into human bestiality. What path should I take to convey most clearly the contrasting intermingling of experiences of pleasure, which projects us outside ourselves, and filth, which belittles us? Perhaps this one: on some plane journeys I like looking out over desert landscapes. Being shut up in the cabin on a long-haul flight promotes a general sloppiness among the passengers, and in that promiscuity, you end up exchanging the smells of musty armpits and overheated feet with those sitting next to you. The feeling of wonderment I have if I have an opportunity to look over a stretch of Siberia or the Gobi Desert is all the greater if I am shackled not so much by my seat belt as by the soupy bath in which I am submerged.

In the Office

I feel a need to suture the cut between the interior and the exterior of my body. Without going so far as a frank anality, I have a facility for finding appeasement in filth: some of the traits of my sexual personality support slight regressive tendencies. I would add to that my habit of completing the sexual act in a maximum number of spots in my familiar space. Some of these places allow a couple to express the urgency of their desire and, at the same time, to experiment with unusual positions, between the elevator and the door to the apartment, in the bath or on the kitchen table. Some of the most exciting locations are in the workplace. Here intimate space and public space meet. One friend whom I used to meet in his office, overlooking the rue de Rennes, would happily let himself be sucked off in front of the floor-to-ceiling window, and the euphoric activity in that part of Paris, which bubbled up to me from the street as I knelt silhouetted against this window, must have contributed to my pleasure. In cities, deprived of distant horizons, I like being able to look out from a window or balcony while I keep a languorous dick captive in a secret place. At home my gaze roams over the narrow courtyard and the neighboring windows; from an office I once worked in on the boulevard Saint-Germain, I contemplated the vast facade of the Ministry of Foreign Affairs. I have also mentioned some of these places when I spoke of the exquisite fear of exposing oneself to involuntary witnesses. To this exhibitionist temptation, I could add the impulse to mark one's territory as an animal would. Like a lemur, which marks out its chosen space with a few jets of urine, you leave a few drops of come on a staircase or the office carpet, you impregnate the storeroom where everyone hangs up their coats. By inscribing this terrain with the act in which a body exceeds its limits, you appropriate it for yourself by osmosis. And you take it from others. There is, without doubt, a degree of provocation or even of indirect aggression toward others in this operation. Our freedom seems all the greater when we claim it in a place where professional cohabitation usually imposes rules and limitations, even if you share that place with the most discreet and tolerant people. Not to mention the fact that we can to some extent embroil them without their knowledge by annexing their belongings into our most private spheres: a sweater they forgot which you park your buttocks on, or the hand towel in the office bathroom which you use to wipe between your legs. There are some places that I have occupied in this way, and I have felt more at home in them than those who spent the best part of their active time there, because I had left the damp outline of my buttocks in the place where they laid out their work and their files. This didn't stop me from entertaining the idea that they, too, might have subverted the role of their workspace, and that we were fucking in one another's wake.

I have methodically laid out the markers of a sexual territory within a professional location. Some places lend themselves particularly well, such as a photographic darkroom or those windowless rooms in which bundles of newspapers are usually kept. The first is closed off by a blackout curtain. It is so small that you have to stay standing, bathed in cabaret light. The light makes the skin look soft as velvet, and this optical impression exacerbates the touch; you only need to brush your hands lightly over each other. Especially as you feel disembodied: the red light makes pale skin almost transparent and swallows up the darker areas, hair or one's clothes.

In a storeroom the most unsettling thing is choosing a place. The area carved up into parallel alleys by the shelving is perfectly uniform, you are no less sheltered from intruders in one alley than another, and you would anyway be seen through the blank spaces between the piles of paper. The net result is that you settle in this place of accumulation as arbitrarily as you would in an empty space, and not before you have turned and looked about you a few times. In this sort of place, fellatio was preferable for me as the act that was easiest to interrupt. I think that it was to do with the gloominess of the place. In a wood, on a deserted track, in any sort of public place, there is always a good reason to choose to hide behind this clump of trees, or in that doorway, either because it offers the greatest comfort or safety, or because it has some playful or aesthetic quality. But here there was none of that. So your stop here was necessarily brief because you could just as easily move a few meters away and migrate from place to place. I would add to that the fact that, if we are happy to be caught in flagrante delicto in a picturesque setting, there would be something almost humiliating about being caught somewhere as ugly as that.

I like the atmosphere of a deserted office, there is a feeling of calm that represents not an end of activity, merely a suspension of it. The harassment of the workday is over, but it still threatens in the shape of a telephone ringing persistently, the gaping jaw of a computer monitor, a file left open. All the tools, all the materials and all the space at my disposal—and mine alone—give me the illusory but calming impression that I have an unlimited capacity for work. As I have already said, when others vacate space, they also vacate time, and it is as if I have all eternity at my disposal to learn how to use every piece of equipment, and to analyze and resolve every problem; it is as if the very fact that I can go into an office without having to introduce myself or apologize smooths out my fitful, halting life. In these situations, and when I was joined in my solitary pursuit by a colleague who doubled as a sexual partner, I only occasionally made use of the relative comfort of the carpet. Worktables were more commonly my platforms. You might think it was because that position, with the woman sitting on the edge of a table and the man standing between her legs, is easier to modify if a colleague should burst into the room. This is not so. It was actually because the movements flowed naturally. Vincent used to make up the dummies, and he and I would sometimes stand side by side looking through the page layouts, not thinking to sit down because he was a man in a hurry and perhaps because we felt we could evaluate them better with an extra thirty centimeters' distance. The slightest hesitation in the flow of our work, and I would turn around. One quick hop, and with my buttocks next to the dummies, my pubis was at the right level. And the level matters. Quite often the best moment to slip from a professional discussion to a silent embrace corresponds to a lapse in concentration, when, for example, you need to look for a document in a bottom drawer. As I bend over to get it, I push out my buttocks. All they want is to be grasped by two firm hands. Then they need a desk to lean on; I am always very cautious if I have to clear everything aside to lie on my back. But not all work surfaces are at the correct height, many are too low, and there are some desks I never went back to a second time. One graphic designer I used to go to see at his agency had cleverly addressed the problem by acquiring pedestal chairs whose height can be adjusted to the nearest centimeter. I would sit down on it in front of him, my genitals exactly opposite his. We had arranged to have a table behind him for me to put my feet on. We could stay like that for a long time without either of us tiring; for me it was like lying in a deck chair, while he rolled his supple waist as if twirling a hula hoop. Intermittently he would substitute his own movement with that of the chair seat, grabbing it with both hands and swinging it fluidly from side to side.

Taboos

I have rarely worried about being caught in flagrante delicto. In the above pages, I have referred several times to the awareness of risk if you undertake a sexual occupation in a place not intended for that purpose, because this awareness also contributes to the pleasure. Even so, the risk is almost always calculated, limited by implicit conventions: someone used to the Bois could draw a map of the places that are out of bounds but where the act is nevertheless possible, and those where it would definitively be impossible; and I have hardly ever made use of offices except outside working hours . . . In a rather prosaic way, the conviction that sexuality, whatever form it may take, is the most widely shared thing in the world, reassures me that nothing unpleasant will happen. An involuntary witness to a sexual act (if he is not driven to join in) would still be sufficiently confused by his own impulses to show no reaction, to maintain a discreet reserve. Jacques who, with a smile, worries about what would have happened if the young backpacker who had just greeted us had passed us two minutes earlier—when, that is, we had our trousers around our ankles and our bucking bodies rustled the leaves by the side of the path, making exactly the same noise as some little animal running for cover. I say nothing would have happened.

I would add that I fear only those I know too well, not the anonymous who mean nothing to me, and I don't think I am alone in this. In this area, the taboo for me would be to use the home you share with someone else while that person was out and unaware of what was going on. Early one afternoon Claude came home to the apartment—a big bourgeois apartment we had just moved into—and into the spare bedroom near the front door. He interrupted a copulation I had not been able to resist. It was the first time that, not in a group session, I had had the full benefit of Paul's large body, which crushed me most pleasurably. Claude went back out without a word. I saw Paul stand up, his back filling the door frame, his naked buttocks proportionately so small as he followed Claude. Through the door I heard him say: "I'm sorry, old man." I was struck by the unaffected tone he used to express his genuine discomfort. I, on the other hand, even though I had already fucked Paul in front of Claude, and even though Claude never referred to the incident, couldn't think about it without feeling persistent guilt for a very long time. At least I could see the spare room as relatively neutral territory. Our shared bedroom, the "conjugal" bed, was absolutely out of bounds. On one occasion the deliquescence of my entire body and of my will (which I have already mentioned, as I have my fatal reaction to a man's first touch) led me to the threshold of that room, the room that is still ours, Jacques's and mine. But I found I couldn't even lean against the door frame, unconsciously afraid that I would release the spring of a trap. So I had to hop backward because the man kneeling in front of me and trying to get to the mound under my skirt had automatically put one of my legs over his shoulder. I lost my balance at the foot of the bed. His incredulous face stared at me through the V of my upturned legs. I brought an end to the exercise and got back to my feet aloofly.

These are the limits set by a morality that belongs more to the realms of superstition than to a clear understanding of what would be right and what would be wrong. First, these limits or markers send signals in only one direction; I have never had any scruples in someone else's bathroom about using her perfumed soap to chase away the fetid residue of the night. Then, I may have cheated on someone in a way that, if and when it was revealed, might have hurt him much more than finding that I had cavorted in his sheets with someone else. I appropriate to other people the same adherence to environment that I have myself, which makes every intimate thing—or anything that has served an intimate purpose—a sort of extension of the body, a sensitive prosthesis. If, while someone is away, you touch something that he touches, he himself is involved by his proximity to it. During an orgy, my tongue could easily lick a pussy that had just been ejaculated into by a man who had first been turned on with me, but the thought of drying myself on a towel that some woman who came clandestinely to my home may have used to wipe between her thighs, or the thought that Jacques might use the same one as some guest of mine whose visit he knew nothing about, horrifies me as much as an epidemic of leprosy. What is more, as a precursor to this fear itself, a hierarchy is established in my mind, granting greater importance to a respect for physical integrity (everything attached to it and that I attach to it) than for moral serenity, because I consider it more irremediable to damage the first than the second. Although I have managed to relativize this theory, I tend to think that we "cope" better with an invisible wound than an external wound. I am a formalist.

Trusting

There is a paradox with respect to this character trait, and that is that, even though images have such a dominant role in my life and even though my eyes guide me far more than

any other organ, during the sexual act, it is as if I am blind.
You could say that on the continuum of the world of sex, I
move like a cell within its tissue. The nocturnal outings, and
the fact of being surrounded, carried and penetrated by shadows suit me well. Better still, I can follow my partner blindly.
I put myself in his hands, abandoning my free will; his presence keeps anything bad from happening to me. When I was
with Éric, we could drive for ages toward some destination
unknown to me, I could end up in the middle of nowhere or
three stories down in an underground parking lot, I never
asked any questions. When all was said and done, whatever
happened was less strange than nothing happening at all.

I have bad memories of the basement of a Moroccan restaurant, near the Place Maubert, not an area we often went
to. There were couches and low tables dotted about in the
chilly room under the vaulted ceiling. We had dined there
alone, me with my breasts bared and my skirt hitched right
up. Each time the waiter or the man I thought was the owner
brought dishes over, Éric would push my top a bit farther aside
and run his hand insistently under my skirt. I remember less
about the heavy and not altogether friendly way these two
men looked at me than I do the way they touched me, quickly,
sporadically, on my companion's tacit invitation. It was I
who brought the waiting to an end by burying Éric's organ
in my mouth. Surely my intention was to escape the less than
friendly attentions of the staff. We left the restaurant without finishing our meal. Were the usual customers not there?
Did Éric know the place well, and hadn't he overestimated
the welcome we might receive? I felt more apprehensive than
if I had been in some incongruous place and a herd of strangers

had set upon me with their dicks hanging out. With Éric I always knew that anyone that we met, in whatever circumstances, could, on some imperceptible sign from him, open my thighs and slip in his member. I didn't think there could be any exceptions to this, as if Éric was a sort of universal ferryman, not to take me across to some promised land but to let people penetrate me, one after another. Hence my uneasiness that evening.

In the undefined places where I met people whose diverse social backgrounds were leveled by a sexual egalitarianism, I was never confronted with any threats or violence; I was even gratified with a degree of attention that I didn't always find in a classic two-person relationship. As for any fear of the police, there was no such thing. On one hand, I have a childlike trust in the ability of the man I am with to ensure our safety—and, in fact, there was never a single incident. On the other hand, even though I feel overcome with shame when a conductor asks me rather rudely for a ticket I have temporarily lost, I would have been only a little put out if I had been caught in the act on the highway. The body discovered by the representative of the law would have been no more or less than the body penetrated by the stranger in the Bois, not so much an inhabited body as a shell from which I had withdrawn. This reckless lack of concern is also at the root of the determination and perseverance I can display during the act, and—indeed—other activities, and is not unrelated to the dissociation that I have just mentioned: either the conscience is annihilated by that determination and can no longer view the act with any distance; or, quite the opposite, when the body is surrendered to automatic functions, the conscience escapes and loses any association with that act. At times like this, no external factor can disturb my body or my partner's, because nothing exists outside the space they occupy. And how small that space is! You rarely fuck expansively in a public place. You tend instead to burrow into each other.

There are few places that have as many forbidden areas as a museum: the works themselves are roped off, and there are plenty of places from which the public is banned. The visitor makes his progress with a vague sense that there is another parallel world that he cannot see but from which he is being watched. Henri, myself and a friend called Fred therefore took advantage of a door that had exceptionally been left ajar at the end of a vast, momentarily deserted gallery in the Museum of Modern Art in Paris. We slipped in behind a flimsy partition wall that hid the pandemonium of what I imagine was a temporary storeroom. We didn't go far into the room. It was very cluttered; but we made up our minds quickly, without thinking it over. Still, I could see the shaft of light on the floor, because we had left the door as it was while I formed a bridge between the two men. After a few minutes they changed places. They both came, one in my cunt, the other in my mouth. I don't know which one of them intermittently suspended the action of his prick to run his hand under my stomach and pleasure me. It encouraged me to do it myself and to set off my own orgasm while the shrinking prick still lingered in my cunt and the other, whose come I had swallowed, had moved away to free me from one of my moorings the better to enjoy my pleasure. This led to a little conversation about the way I masturbated. I explained, believing that I was revealing something astonishing, that in less

precarious circumstances I could have had two or three con-
secutive orgasms. They made fun of me. That was very common for a woman, they claimed, as we slowly tucked our shirts
back into our trousers. When we went back out into the light,
the museum was just as empty. We went on looking around
the exhibition. I went from one painting to another, and from
Henri to Fred for their comments, and this visit was all the
more enjoyable because it was bolstered by the complicity that
from then on would link me to those two men and to that
place.

In the dark storeroom, with my body bent double between two other bodies and my eyes staring vertically down,
I was completely hemmed in. I am convinced that when my
field of vision is limited, then in some primitive way, this
provokes anything that could threaten me or simply upset
me—in fact, anything that I don't want to countenance for
one reason or another. The body of whomever I am with becomes an obstacle, and whatever lies beyond it that I cannot
see doesn't really exist. So, in the position I was in at the
museum, only this time on the first floor of a shop selling
sadomasochist gear on the boulevard de Clichy—again in a
stock room—I have one cheek pressed up against Éric's
tummy while he holds me by my shoulders and the owner of
the boutique grasps my rear end, ramming me back and forth
on his dick. Before assuming this position, I notice that the
man is very small and thickset with short arms, but as soon
as he disappears from view, his person disintegrates—so much
so that I address my request to Éric for the man to put on a
condom before penetrating. The man is perturbed by this
request and forced to rummage through some boxes; he ad-

mits quietly that he is afraid his wife might come in. Even though he has a thick organ that has to force entry, he hovers in limbo the whole time. A girl who looks like a shy employee watches the entire scene rather sullenly. From time to time I catch her eye as I glance sideways; her eyes are black, probably ringed with kohl. I feel as if I am on a stage, separated by some indistinct void from a gloomy spectator waiting for the action to start. When I look at her, I am in some ways looking back at myself, and I end up seeing myself, but just the head, the neck hunched back into the shoulders, the cheek crushed against Éric's jacket and scuffed by the zipper, the mouth is open, whereas what is going on above the waist is part of a sort of backdrop. The dwarf's pokes became as unreal to me as a sound heard thundering from the wings of a theater, to imply some far-off action.

Another time, in a sauna, it was the friendliness of a little masseuse that brought about this duality. The tiers of slatted wooden benches had forced me to keep turning around. I had alternately bent and reached up to take all the eager pricks in my mouth. I don't sweat much. So I stayed dry long enough for each of them to grab hold of me, while I myself had to make great efforts to hold on to and direct pieces of flesh that had become viscous and slippery. All the way to the showers, they worried at my clitoris and pinched my nipples. Eventually I lay down aching on the massage table. The girl spoke softly, leaving a pause between her sentences in the same way that she stopped to put talc on her hands between each series of movements. She was sympathizing with my fatigue: *When you feel like that, there's nothing quite like a sauna followed by a good massage, is there!* She feigned ignorance of exactly what sort of ordeals I had just subjected my body to, and she spoke to me as a beautician would, offering professional but also maternal ministrations to a modern active woman who without reserve puts herself into her hands. I have always liked slipping into a role, especially in this sort of situation, and I replied to her questions, relaxing more by this conformism than by the action of her fingers. It amused me to feel her kneading muscles that a few moments earlier, had been subjected to more carnal pressures. She also seemed distant. I was separated from her by a succession of transformations. She took on a disguise constructed by the course of our conversation, but beneath this disguise was my skin, which she touched so gently, overlaying the other caresses that had gone before, and I abandoned this skin to her just as willingly, like an old castoff. After all, I was no more the debauched little bourgeoise she must have taken me for than the steadfast one we were inventing. As far as I know, we were the only two women in the establishment that evening, but I thought of myself as being in the active realm of the men—and, in a way, they were still standing around me—whereas I saw her in a passive feminine realm, a place she occupied as an observer, and the two were incontrovertibly separate.

In the end, the selection operated by my sight is intensified by the assured protection of my partner's gaze, by the veil with which he covers me, a veil that is of course both opaque and transparent. Jacques does not tend to choose the busiest places to take pictures of me naked—he would only show me off in the photo—but he has a predilection for places one passes through, and more particularly for the transitory nature of the things you find in them (the carcasses of abandoned cars, pieces of furniture, ruins), which took us to the places where these things are used. We are cautious. I always wear a dress that is easy to button back up. In the frontier station of Port-Bou, we wait until the platform is empty. There is a train pulling out, but it is two or three platforms away. Anyway, the people are far too busy to notice us, and we make sure that the three or four frontier guards are still chatting with one another. I am looking into the light, so I can't really make out the signs Jacques is giving me. I start walking toward him with the dress open right down the front. I gain confidence as I go. Hypnotized by the fluttering of the silhouette waiting for me at the far end, I feel as if I am carving out my own channel as I go, opening up the acrid, laden air to form a space no wider than the gap between my two swinging arms. Each click of the camera confirms the impunity of my advance. When I reach the end, I lean against the wall. Jacques takes a few more pictures. More nonchalance is authorized once the open space is behind me. The euphoria of a conquest: we were no more interrupted in the underpass that links the platforms, or in the large, empty, echoing concourse, or on the little terrace that one of the station entrances opened out onto, a place invaded by cats and graced with a fountain.

The second photographic session of the day takes place in the sailors' cemetery, in the walkways between the rows of family graves built in several stories, on Benjamin's tomb, in a game of hide-and-seek with two or three women walking slowly to visit graves. It seems obvious to me to be naked in the sea air and among the dead. But I feel unsure about being in that ambiguous place, which is both open to all and profoundly private, standing between the horizon and the framing lens. It is not the balustrade that holds me safe above the drop but his eyes on me, alternately driving me on and following me, his gaze unfurling between us like an anchor. When I face the sea and turn my back on the camera so that I am no longer aware of how far it is from me, then the lens seems to attach itself to my shoulders and the small of my back, drawing me in with a powerful suction.

After supper we go back to the car, which is parked near the cemetery. Now we make the most of the evening light for some frottage, ass against fly. My undressing requires that we up the stakes; having done nothing but unbutton and undress, I want to open myself up wide again. I am half lying on the hood, and my cunt is getting ready to swallow the end of his prick when the air is sliced by violent barking. A furious little dog crosses the halo of light around the only streetlamp, a man hobbling along behind him. Brief moment of confusion: I push the skirt of my dress back down, Jacques manages as best he can to stow his now unpliable parts. Still stroking him through the thickness of his trousers, I insist that we watch which way the man goes because, as if this was meant to happen, he is now pacing up and down watching us out of the corner of his eye. Jacques decides it would be better to go home. In the car, in the state of panic I am always in when very frustrated, I am overcome with anger. I counter Jacques's cautious comments by saying the man might have come and joined us. Exasperated desire is a naive dictator that cannot believe anyone would oppose it or even inconvenience it. Isn't it also that I feel I have been abandoned by the extreme attentiveness that has followed me and protected me all day and that was, to some extent, my link with the world? My anger derives from a sense of powerlessness. When my need to be penetrated is thwarted, I am torn between these two conflicting states: on the one hand, an incredulity that means I cannot understand the reasons (however reasonable they may be) why my partners aren't responding to my imperious waiting; and on the other hand, an equally stupid inability to break down their resistance (however circumstantial, definitive or wavering it may be), in other words, to take the initiative by making some seductive or provocative gesture that would make them change their minds. I wait stubbornly, exhaustingly, for some initiative on the other's part which they may never take. How many times have I resented Jacques when the urge came to me while doing something quite ordinary, some domestic chore, for example, but I didn't let it show and somehow felt reproachful toward him for failing to read the circumvolutions of my brain where the source of my libido lies. If I can be forgiven for drawing a parallel with a situation that bears no comparison with these capricious outbursts of mine, I would compare it to the state of someone who, since birth or as a result of an accident, doesn't have the use of his limbs or the power of speech, but whose intelligence and need to communicate remain intact. He depends entirely on what around him to break through his isolation. It is said that this entourage can have some degree of success if they pay minute attention to the subtlest signals, such as blinking, from the patient, or by massaging him patiently to awaken his nerve endings. Sexual frustration plunges me into what I would call a benign autism, which makes me utterly dependent on the twinkle of lust in someone else's eye and the caresses he has the goodness to offer me. On that condition, my anxiety dissipates and I can reclaim my place in an environment that is no longer hostile to me.

On the way home, I ask to stop on the shoulder. But my anger only increases because we are on a busy main road and it really wouldn't be possible. So I cut myself off from the road and the car. I concentrate all my attention on my pubis, which I thrust forward, and become absorbed in a slow, circular stroking movement of the sort of sticky little animal that lives there. From time to time the headlights of oncoming cars light up my stomach, as smooth as porcelain. What sort of mirage am I burying myself in then? Surely not a continuation of the events that were left in suspense a few minutes earlier. That particular business is over. No, I prefer taking refuge in one of my reassuring old scenarios, a long way away from where I actually am. In an intense, sustained effort of concentration, I construct the scene in great detail, perhaps the one in which I am pulled to pieces by countless fingering hands on a stretch of wasteland or in the toilets of a fleabag theater—I don't really remember. When Jacques stretches out his arm without taking his eyes off the road and traces blind, sweeping movements over my breasts and stomach, and when he dives his hand down to fight mine and gain possession of its soaking little toy, he upsets the seamlessness of the scene. I resist the urge to stop him.

As we come into Perpignan, Jacques parks the car in a brightly lit, empty parking lot at the foot of a block of apartments. In order to get close to me and because of the gap between the seats, he has to throw his chest forward like a gargoyle. His head comes into my field of vision and eclipses everything. He plunges into me with three or four vigorous fingers. I like hearing the smacking sound of my wet labia; the frankness of this noise wakes me from my fantasies. I never stretch out my body to offer it up to these caresses straightaway or that easily. Before I give in and spread my thighs wide, before I throw my head back and open up my arms to offer up my breasts, I need some time. Time, perhaps, to uncoil from the curled position I automatically assume, the position imprinted on my body when, as a child, I had to hide my masturbating; time to accept, as usual and once again (and even after maneuvering in front of a camera for hours), showing my body all at once in its entirety. It is not nudity that I am afraid of—quite the contrary—it is the snapshot moment of revelation. And it is even less because I hesitate to abandon myself to others—absolutely the contrary!—it is that I don't know how to move from my introspective vision to seeing myself. In fact, to achieve it I first need the other's gaze. I can't say: "There, look!" I would rather wait till he says, not without caution: "Look how I look at you."

I let Jacques get on with it. But as I really do seem to have taken refuge somewhere deep inside me, in order to return to reality, I have to pass through a sort of fetal state. I curl to grab the hardened member so my lips can feel the soft envelope that slides over its axis. I can mobilize myself into this act so utterly that I feel full up to the brim, my entire body has been put on and filled out like a glove.

. . .

In a series of images taken by an American photographer who published some of them many years later in the magazine *On Seeing*, I can be seen—I can see myself today—first standing like a fragile sleepwalker (almost as if I am swaying) next to a couple fornicating on a mattress. It is dark, it looks as if I am dressed entirely in black, the light falls only on the girl's knees and the soles of the boy's feet. In other shots I am sitting next to the couple, bent in two; you can just make out, under a curtain of hair, that my head is squeezed between the girl's thigh and the boy's hips. I must be trying to lick whatever parts of their conjoined genitals I can reach. What do I look like? A conscientious workman—plumber, decorator, mechanic—examining the areas where his intervention is needed; a child whose toy has rolled under the bed and who searches the darkness to find it; an exhausted runner who sits down and drops his chest forward before catching his breath. I can confirm that the effort I put into introducing my body into the space between their two bodies (and you could be forgiven for thinking I want to insert it whole) is matched by intense mental concentration.

4. Details

I really like sucking men's cocks. I was initiated in this at virtually the same time I learned to direct the exposed glans toward the other, subterranean entrance. In my naïveté I initially thought that a blow job was a deviant sexual practice. I can still hear myself describing the thing to a dubious and slightly disgusted girlfriend; I tried to affect indifference when I was actually rather proud of my discovery and my aptitude for it. This aptitude is very difficult to explain because, over and above whatever vestiges there may be of the oral stage, and before the challenge put into accomplishing an act that you believe to be abnormal, there is an obscure identification with the member you appropriate. During an exploration carried out simultaneously with fingers and tongue, you come to know every last detail of its topography and even its tiniest reactions—perhaps better than its owner himself. As a result there is a feeling of ineffable mastery: a tiny quivering of the end of the tongue, and you unleash a disproportionate response. Added to this is the fact that taking something right into your mouth gives you a more thorough feeling of being filled than when it is the vagina that is occupied. The feeling in the vagina is diffuse, radiating outward, the occupant seems to melt there; whereas you can perfectly distinguish the gentle proddings of the glans with the inside or the outside of the lips, on the tongue, the palate and even in the throat. Not to mention the fact that, in the final phase, you taste the sperm. In short, you are touched as subtly as you yourself touch. But for me there still remains the mystery of the transmission of sensation from the anterior orifice to the posterior one. How is it that the effects of sucking can be felt by the other end of the body, that the way the lips squeezing around the penis causes a rigid bracelet to form around the mouth of the vagina? When I perform fellatio really well, taking my time, at leisure to adjust my position and vary my rhythm, I can feel an impatience rising from some source within my body, flowing and concentrating enormous muscular energy in that place of which I have only a vague image, on the edge of this abyss that opens me up so overwhelmingly. The aperture of a barrel ringed with steel. When the ring is forged by the spreading arousal of the nearby clitoris, I can understand it. But when the order comes from the mouth!

The explanation undoubtedly lies in some detour via the mind. Even though I may have my eyes closed most of the time, they are so close to this meticulous work that I *see* all the same, and the image I have of it is a powerful activator of my desire. The fantasy may also revolve around the fact that, lying just behind the eyes, the brain has perfect and instantaneous intelligence of the thing so nearly touching it. First of all, I see the actions that determine my breathing: the flexible channel of my hand, my lips folded over my teeth so as not to hurt my tongue, which quickly dabs the glans as it comes closer. I evaluate their progress visually, the whole hand moving with the lips, sometimes with a slight twisting movement, and increasing the pressure when it reaches the thicker bud at the end. Then suddenly the hand goes its own way to rub swiftly up and down, forming a pincer with just two fingers, making the silky tip bob against the cushioned surface of my lips, pursed into a kiss. Jacques always lets out a brief, clear little "ha" of surprised delight (even though he knows the maneuver perfectly well)—which redoubles my own excitement—when the hand releases its grip, allowing the organ to disappear to the back of my throat. I try to keep it there for a moment and even to maneuver its rounded tip over the back of my palate until tears come to my eyes, until I'm suffocating. Or—but for this you need your whole body to be well balanced—I hold the hub still and gravitate my whole head around it, distributing gentle strokes from my cheeks, my chin moistened with saliva, my forehead, hair and even the end of my nose. I lick lavishly right down to the balls, which you can take into your mouth whole. These movements are punctuated by longer halts on the glans, where the tip of the tongue describes circles, unless it decides instead to devote itself to niggling at the edge of the foreskin. Then, bang! Without any warning I take the whole thing back into my mouth and I hear the cry, which transmits its wave down to the cast-iron ring forged around the entry to my cunt.

It would be easy for me to write pages about this, especially as just describing this painstaking job has already triggered the first signs of excitement. There might even be a distant link between my attention to detail in a blow job and the care I take over each description in my writing. I will restrict myself to adding that I also like giving up my role as the driving force. I like to have my head held still by two firm hands and to be fucked in my mouth the way I can be fucked in my cunt. In general, I feel the need to take a man into my mouth in the first few moments of a sexual encounter, just to titillate those few milliliters of blood that produce the erection. Either we are standing and I let myself drop down at my partner's feet, or we are lying down and I quickly make my way under the sheet. It is like a game: I go into the dark looking for the thing I want. And in fact, in these moments, I have a silly tendency to talk like a greedy child. I ask for my "big lollipop," and it gives me a kick. And when I lift my head up, because I do have to relax the muscles sucked in along the insides of my cheeks, I stick to the "Umm . . . it's good" of someone establishing that her taste buds are enjoying something she is eating. By the same token, I receive all compliments with the same vanity as a good pupil on prize day. Nothing phases me more than hearing that I give "the best blow jobs." Better than that: when, with a view to writing this book, I talk to a friend twenty-five years after my sexual relationship with him ended and I hear him say that he has "never met a girl who could suck a man off so well," I lower my eyes, in some ways out of modesty, but also to hide my pride. It is not that I have been deprived of other forms of gratification in my personal or professional life, but as far as I can see, there is a balance to be sustained between the acquisition of moral and intellectual qualities that earn the respect of our peers, and a proportional excellence in practices that flout these qualities, brush them aside and deny them. We can demonstrate this ability to such an extent that we wouldn't mind seeing the admiration it inspires turning to mockery. Éric nearly punched one narrow-minded idiot we met one evening in the club called the Cleopatra. When I was offered something to drink, the idiot—who wasn't able to appreciate my enthusiasm in a fitting manner—announced that it was about time because it was beginning to "smell of burned rubber."

The Body in Pieces

If each of us drew our own body as if by dictation from our own internal perspective, we would produce a real gallery of monsters! I myself would be hydrocephalic and callipygian, and these two protuberances would be joined by an insubstantial mollusklike arm (I have trouble making my breasts count for anything), and the whole thing would be planted on two posts that impede movement more than they facilitate it (I have had a complex about my legs for a long time). Perhaps it's my cerebral nature that has led me to accord priority to the organs of the head, the eyes and the mouth. There could even be a compensatory relationship between them. When I was very young, people used to compliment me on my big eyes; people noticed them because they were dark brown. As I grew up, my eyes became proportionately less important within my face, and when I was an adolescent, my wounded narcissism had to accept that no one made much fuss about them any more. So I made my mouth, which I thought was rather nice, a possible means of attraction. And I learned to open it wide, and to close my eyes at the same time, at least in certain circumstances, while my backside came to represent the image I had of myself, its rotundity all the more accentuated by my pronounced waist. This backside that I extend ever farther into the unknown regions of the *outback* (the name Australians give to the desert that lies behind them), which I will never see. Jacques once gave me a postcard of a sketch Picasso made for *Les Demoiselles d'Avignon:* a woman seen from behind, her torso the shape of an isosceles triangle, her buttocks curving dramatically above what look like knuckles of ham. My portrait, he said.

My ass is another side of who I am. Claude used to say, "so-so face, but what an ass!" I like it when Jacques is on the job and he uses the word "ass" unspecifically to designate the whole lower part of my body, which he is penetrating, and when he accompanies his declarations of love addressed to it with sharp slaps on my buttocks. I make a point of asking for this sort of attention. "Rub my ass" is one of my most frequent requests. In response, he grabs my buttocks and shakes their malleable mass as if he were trying to whip up two mountains of cream. If he finishes the job by inserting two fingers in a duck's-head formation and then opens the bill—i.e., parts the two fingers—in the narrow corridor that leads from the parting of the buttocks to the opening of the cunt, then I just can't wait for his cock a minute longer.

Once he is inside me, I, too, can get going. Whether I am lying down or on all fours, I play energetically on the suppleness of my waist, and the repercussions of my regular, vigorous thrusts provoke the fantastical melding of my mouth and my genitals. I want to know whether I am "sucking" him well with my cunt. "Am I going to suck up all your come?" The answer I hope for subsumes my identity into that part of me in which all of me is concentrated: "Oh, Catherine! Your ass, your ass . . ." Knowing that what I cannot see is being attentively examined is just as stimulating. A focused ray of light (from an adjustable bedside lamp, for example) is preferable to more diffuse lighting. I have been known to suggest using a flashlight. By glancing back, I can see the expression on a man's face as he scrutinizes the cleft between my buttocks which facilitates the disappearance of his precious appendage. I rely heavily on the description he gives me, however literal and crude it may be. "You have a good view of my ass?" "Oh, yes, it's gorgeous, you know, it's really swallowing my dick. Oh, the bitch wants more . . ." If there happens to be a mirror nearby, if I put myself in profile, I can oversee the immersion and emergence of what looks like a piece of flotsam tossed by the swell. Because of this predilection for sensations in my rump, the doggie position has been my favorite for a long time, until I ended up admitting to myself—we always end up being sexually honest with ourselves, but this can, of course, take a long time—that, even though it allowed the rod to strike deep and hard, it still wasn't the form of penetration that satisfied me the most. In other words, having gone in pursuit of the dick with the energetic buckings of my hips, and having been alternately pinned down and buffed like a polisher's duster, I like to be turned over and nailed in the classic position.

The pleasure I take in exposing my ass goes back a long time. When I was six or seven, I would expose it to my brother in a game that included some of the moves I used to masturbate. That is, with my skirt hitched up, I would crease my panties up into the front of my crack, and I would push my buttocks out as far as I could beyond the back of the small bench I was sitting on. Then I would wait for the little guy to go behind me. What amused us about it was that I would pretend to have revealed myself quite absentmindedly, and he pretended to brush my buttocks inadvertently.

It must be that we give caresses in the way that we receive them because I have always responded eagerly to men with sensitive asses. I have mentioned the friend who offered himself on all fours for me to finger-fuck until my arm and shoulder were paralyzed with pain. Another one planted his buttocks on my nose without any warning. At the beginning of our relationship, he was being coy and I had to overcome his resistance before I could undertake fellatio. But I had hardly taken him into my mouth when his body stiffened and he pivoted around and presented me with two resolute buttocks. It was easier for me to get to his asshole than his glans. Even so, when I got back up, I thought he still wore the same severe, almost reproving, expression that he had assumed when I first took him in my mouth. After that, I got into the habit of exploring this man's body in minute detail; I have never licked, kissed and nibbled anyone so thoroughly, from his earlobes to the shifting skin attaching his testicles, via the delicate depressions under his arms, in the crooks of his elbows and in the folds of his groin. It was the systematic occupation of a territory where I left my mark in the form of tiny gobs of spit released from a few centimeters to give the limpid saliva time to stretch out, soiling where I had passed.

Is it because people were less interested in my bosom that it is more lymphatic by nature, and is it because I never thought to offer it spontaneously to be seen and fondled by others that I find it tedious having to stimulate my partner's nipples? A lot of men ask you to "do their tits" and they even expect this coaxing to take the form of pinching and biting these delicate areas. I have regularly been reproached for not pinching hard enough when my hand hurt from rolling nipples between my fingers, at the same time trying to squeeze them. Not only is the sadistic the least developed of my impulses, I can't find any resonance in myself for pleasure provoked in this way. Personally, I prefer my breasts to be enveloped in a wider, more subtle gesture, which is even nicer at the time in my cycle when my breasts are heavier because then I can feel them quivering gently. I don't like them to be pressed or pinched. Any fussing over my nipples I keep for myself, and then only to feel how hard and rough they are under my smooth palms. But in my own intimacy, I can experience an even more striking contrast: kneeling or on all fours, I rub my breasts on my thighs, and this is a confusing feeling; it feels as if my own thighs are strangers to me, as if they don't belong to me, that their touch comes from outside me, and I melt, always surprised by their velvety skin.

On the subject of seeking out a contrast between rough surfaces and soft ones, I have just remembered one of the first times I experienced an erotic emotion as such. My brother and I would be sent to spend a holiday with some friends of our father's whose numerous grandchildren played with us. One day, the grandfather, who was ill, had to go to bed and I went to see him in his room. As I sat on the edge of the bed, he started to examine my face. Feeling his way with his fingers, he commented that I had a very fine jawbone; when he reached my neck, he diagnosed that later in life I might be susceptible to goiter. These contradictory observations worried me. Then, slipping his hand under my blouse, he brushed past my breasts, which were barely beginning to bud. And as I stayed there, silent and motionless, he said that when I became a woman, I would really like it when people stroked my "titties" like this. I still didn't move, or perhaps just my head, which I turned toward the wall as if I couldn't hear what I was being told. The callused surface of his big hand snagged on my skin. I was aware for the first time of the stiffening of my nipple. I listened to his predictions. I was suddenly brought to the threshold of womanhood, and I felt a sense of pride. A child forges its power in the enigma of its future life. So, though disconcerted by this gesture, for which I had no prepared response, I turned back to look at this man, whom I was fond of, on his bed. I felt sorry for him because his wife was crippled, obese, her legs covered in suppurating sores that he dressed meticulously morning and evening. At the same time, his grayish face and his lumpy nose made me want to laugh. I extricated myself gently.

That evening, lying in the bed that I shared with one of his granddaughters, I told her about the episode. He had touched her, too. We looked each other right in the eye as we spoke, trying to measure the magnitude of our discovery in the other's gaze. We were pretty sure the grandfather was doing something forbidden, but the secret that he gave us to share was far more valuable than some moral whose meaning was, anyway, no clearer. When I once decided—again, with a sense of pride, almost bravado—to talk about my masturbating in confession, the priest's reaction was so disappointing (he made absolutely no comment and just gave me a few Aves and the odd Pater to recite as usual) that I felt nothing but contempt for him afterward. So, trying to tell him that I had been stirred because an old man had put his hand on my breast . . . !

If I see a man's eyes alighting—even for half a second—on the place where I then deduce that my bra is straining the buttons of my blouse, or, more usually, if I am talking to someone whose staring eyes are apparently following a train of thought unrelated to what I am saying, I always take refuge in exactly the same modest behavior as in that first examination by the grandfather. For the same reason, you won't find any low-cut or tight-fitting dresses in my wardrobe. This modesty extends to even those around me. If I am sitting on the sofa in someone's living room, next to a woman in very revealing clothes, I will instinctively pull down the hem of my own skirt and hunch over to hide my breasts. In this sort of situation, my discomfiture derives as much from the impression that, by association, it is my own anatomy that she is revealing, as from my tendency—described earlier—to break down the barriers of sexual contact from the word go; by adjusting my clothes, I am stopping myself from burying my hands between the two half-exposed breasts and revealing them entirely. And yet I myself wore no underwear at all for many years. I can't remember why I gave it up. It was definitely not to follow the feminists who wanted us all to burn our bras, because I never adhered to that philosophy, but it was perhaps in the same spirit of rejecting accessories of seduction. Obviously, the results could have the opposite of the desired effect; breasts that can be seen moving freely under clothes are just as tantalizing—

although more "naturally"—as those displayed to best effect by a bra. I could at least feel free from any suspicion of having a battle plan for my conquests. I passed up panties in the same way. For how many years was I compelled, for reasons of hygiene, to clean the crotch of my trousers every evening, when it would have been much quicker to put a pair of panties in the washing machine? I just thought it was much simpler to slip all my other clothes on directly. This tendency was dictated to me by a minimalist, almost functionalist principle, according to which a free body need not weigh itself down with ornamentation, as long as it is ready without the need for preliminaries, no shedding of lace or manipulating of bra hooks. In sum, I don't like it when a man undresses me with his eyes, but once you get down to undressing for real, then it might as well be in one swift move.

If a subjective eye were on a journey, what a world of contrasts it would see! Like a mountain road interrupted by tunnels, you pass abruptly from darkness into light, and from light into darkness. Here I am trying to explain that I prefer to keep covered something that it is perfectly acceptable to reveal, when within these same pages I have displayed an intimacy that most people keep secret. It is obvious that, in the same way psychoanalysis helps you to shed unwanted parts of yourself, when you write a book in the first person the latter becomes the third person. The more detailed my descriptions of my body and my actions, the more I leave myself behind. Who recognizes themselves in those magnifying mirrors that show cheeks and noses as vast fissured landscapes? Because sexual pleasure brings you outside your own limits, it can impose the same sort of distance. Perhaps there is even

a structural relationship, and the distance governs the pleasure as much as it is governed by it, at least for the category
of creature to which I belong. Because, and this is the point
I wanted to make, the same woman whom I described as
uncomfortable under someone's insistent gaze, and who hesi-
tates to wear suggestive clothes, the same woman in fact who
partook blindly in sexual adventures with faceless partners,
this same woman, then, takes indisputable pleasure in exposing herself on the condition that the exposure is distanced at
once, by a narrative.

Image and language conspire. It is so stimulating to look
in a mirror and measure—to the nearest centimeter—the
amount of flesh that your own flesh can swallow, and this is
because the show gives rise to words. "Oh my! It's going in
so smoothly, so deep! Hang on, I'm going to leave it there so
that you can really see it, I'll fuck you right, afterward . . . "
One kind of dialogue that Jacques and I adopted willingly
can be characterized by being purely factual. If the vocabulary is crude and limited this has less to do with a desire to
provoke each other by upping the obscenity stakes than a need
to be accurate in our descriptions. "Can you feel how wet I
am? Even my thighs are soaked, and my little clit's all swollen." "God, you move your ass well! Does it want my prick?
Does it?" "Yes, but I want to feel your cock on my clit again
first, can I rub you against it?" "Yes, and afterward we're going
to fuck the ass really good!" "That's good. How about you,
does your dick like it?" "Yes, he likes it." "Is it pulling on your
balls, too?" "Yes, it's pumping them really well. But hey, we're
going to give this cunt another really good thrust, aren't we?"
And so the exchange goes on in a tone of voice that remains,

even as we approach the conclusion, fairly measured. Insofar as we don't see or feel the same thing at the same time, each speaks to the other with the intention of adding to his knowledge. You could also say that we're like two dubbing actors, their eyes riveted on the screen where they watch the actions of the characters to whom they give their voices: with our words, we relay the actions of the protagonists in the porn film we are watching, and whose names are Ass, Cunt, Balls and Prick.

Description cuts bodies into pieces, satisfies the need to fetishize them, to instrumentalize them. That famous scene in Godard's *Le Mépris,* when, word by word, Piccoli runs over Bardot's body, is a beautiful transposition of the two-way traffic between sight and speech, each word bringing into focus a part of the body. How many times people say "Look!" when they're fucking. Of course, you are at your leisure to see things close at hand, but in order to see well, we sometimes also need to stand back, the way we move back from an exhibit in a museum. Undressing, I love to gaze at a promising-looking cock. Abiding by the law of the Gestalt theory, it looks enormous in relation to the body, which becomes almost fragile in its—sometimes laughable—seminudity and its unexpected isolation in the middle of the room; in any event, the cock certainly looks bigger than it would if I was looking at it on its own. In the same way, I can, without any warning, break out of the game and go and stand a couple of meters away, with my back turned, my hands forced onto my buttocks to spread them as far apart as possible, bringing into the same sight line both the brownish crater of the asshole and the crimson valley of the vulva. An invitation become imperative, like a greengrocer saying: "You must taste this fruit," I'm saying "You must look at my ass." And because things are more picturesque if they are animated, I make it quiver.

To show my ass and to see my face. There are few pleasures to equal this double polarity. The layout of the bathroom is perfect: while the basin offers a perfect gripping point to brace the shocks to my rear end, I intermittently catch sight of my harshly lit face in the mirror above it, a face that—quite unlike my lower half, which is totally mobilized—is almost lifeless. The cheeks are hollow and the mouth half open like a windup doll whose mechanism has wound down. It could be the face of a dead woman except for the eyes, which are intolerably listless. I try both to avoid them by lowering my eyelids and to seek out their gaze. That gaze is the anchoring point; it is by seeing its reflection that I establish this certainty: there I am, that is me coming. It is the siphon through which all of me is evacuated: I cannot recognize myself in such a state of release; with a feeling of shame, I reject it. That is how pleasure stays on a knife edge: just as the multiplication of two negative numbers gives a positive number, this pleasure is the product not, as is sometimes said, of an absence from oneself but of the bringing together of this perceived absence and the feeling of horror that it provokes in a flash of conscience. Sometimes I bring myself to this peak of pleasure all by myself, as an interval in my bathroom routine. With one hand on the edge of the basin and the other one masturbating, I watch myself in the mirror out of the corner of my eye.

A particular porn film made quite an impression on me. The man was taking the woman from behind. The camera was facing her so that her face was in the foreground. Thanks to the pressure exerted on her whole body, her face was projected forward and distorted, as things are when they come too close to the lens. You could hear the man's orders: "Look! Look at the camera!" and the girl's eyes looked directly into yours, the viewer's. I thought he might well be pulling her hair to force her to raise her head. This scene has given me a lot of inspiration for the little scenarios that nourish my masturbating. In real life, a man I met only once gave me such intense pleasure that I have very precise memories of the encounter, and this was because with every thrust, he would order me to "Look me in the eye." I did as I was told, knowing that he was witness to the disintegration of my face.

An Ability to Absorb

One weakness of porn films is to present stereotyped images of orgasm; the characters always come after a series of accelerated jerks, eyes closed, mouths open and screaming. Now, orgasms can happen with no movement at all and in silence, and you can watch them building up and then unfold. It is usually when you want to fire up or stimulate desire that—in life as in films—you resort to clichés. Pretty much the same words, obscene or not, come to everyone. Men frequently order partners to ask for them and their organs ("Do you want a big one? Answer me," "Say my name, go on, say it"), whereas women, even the most independent-minded, tend toward subjection, even to the extent of asking for what would be horrible injuries ("Stab it into me!," "Go on, tear me open!"). Seeing myself in a video spreading the come that has just spurted onto me all over my breasts, I wonder whether I am not merely repeating something I have seen dozens of times on the screen. The jet is not as frothy as in the films, but it is nevertheless spectacular; the spunk makes my skin shine. Did men and women use the same rhetoric and was their erotic repertoire the same before the invention of cinema? But the more powerful the orgasm, the less "hamming it up" there is. I can confirm that in my own case. While the level of pleasure is rising, I take a very active part. As well as moving my hips, I use my arms and legs. If I am lying on my back, I spur on my partner by repeatedly kicking my heels on his buttocks and thighs. Then I reach a stage when this frantic level of activity drops. My partner is now concentrating on only one inert parcel of flesh. My voice sounds quite different. We have already abandoned our running commentary, the words we exchange become more laconic. I say "Yes, yes, yes, yes," sometimes accompanying this litany with rapid movements of my head from left to right, or I keep saying "Go on, go on." And suddenly my voice becomes higher, louder, with the clarity and authority of an actor who has learned to project her voice, and the words are more spaced out, the syllables more emphatic, "Keep go-ing." Sometimes the "yes" becomes a "no," and in some images I see myself burying my face in my hands.

I wouldn't do the job that I do, nor would I be capable of gathering together all these notes, if I did not have some gift for observation. A gift put to greater effect because it is coupled with a solid superego. I don't let myself go easily, and in those moments when you are supposed to be completely passive, I am often still alert. I have, therefore, always paid very close attention to my partners, to those who I knew well, of course, but also to any level of relationship, a deep and lasting attachment or a passing affair. This degree of attention surely belongs to the same perceptive structure as the concentration I display in front of a painting, or my ability— in the Métro, a restaurant or a waiting room—to lose myself completely in my contemplation of the people sitting next to me. An attention that defines my acumen. I take pride in the fact that I am quite an expert, and I have become one because I have always been aware of the effects my initiatives produced. As I have described at the beginning of this chapter, I have spontaneously slipped under other people's skin in an effort to feel myself what they were feeling. That is not just a turn of phrase; I have surprised myself by mimicking habits and exclamations that were peculiar to someone else. Which amounts to saying that I often relegated my own pleasure to the background. It took me a long time, a really long time, to identify the caresses, the positions that I liked best. I will venture this as an explanation: I was not from the start granted a body predisposed to pleasure. First I had to give myself—literally abandon my whole body—to sexual activity, to lose myself in it so thoroughly that I confused myself with my partner so that I could emerge from this transformation having sloughed off the mechanical body I was given at birth and taken on a second body, one capable of taking as much as it could give. In the meantime, how many faces and bodies did I lose myself in watching!

With very few exceptions, I can remember with relative accuracy the bodies of my main partners, and even what their faces looked like at the moment when the other part of their being was released. These images are accompanied by memories of the convulsive movements and particular choice of words each of them made. Observation does not automatically lead to judgment, but if it is scrupulous, it keeps the conscience in the realm of objectivity. I may have been seduced by a man's physical beauty, but that wouldn't stop me from identifying flaws that could cut short any fascination for him. For example, a roundish face set off with almond eyes but mounted on a head that was peculiarly flattened at the back, so that when I looked at it in profile, it brought to mind a squashed balloon. A quarter turn and the man whose face could be compared to a Renaissance painting had no more depth than a picture on canvas. If I run back through a portrait gallery, then I can find fault with my memory and my powers of observation: paradoxically, there was one man whose good looks were particularly seductive to me (in fact, the only man of all my sexual contacts who was younger than I), but I have no sexual memories of him. I can call to mind lots of expressions and gestures he made and plenty of things that he said, but not one of them would have occurred while we were fucking!

Was nature trying to spare men the danger of being torn in two when she ordained that, when their muscles are strained to the limits, this tension is compensated by bathing their faces in peace? Doesn't it look as if they are throwing their faces back to refresh them under a fountain in that instant when they come to the end of the pursuit that has exercised their entire body? Many of them adopt this serene expression; not the man who looked like a Renaissance portrait. While there is a whole succession of peaceful faces in my memory—one making a little "o" with his mouth and, because he had a mustache, looking as silly as a child playing dress up; another who smiled so halfheartedly that it could have been a sign of embarrassment, the sort of smile a shy person would wear as he apologized for being caught in some indecent act—or again, another man whose face was usually so smooth, who wore a mask of suppressed pain. He would have seemed pitiable if, in those moments, he hadn't added to the usual exclamation of "I'm coming, I'm coming!" the words "Oh, my God!" A comical invocation I couldn't help noticing.

But calm can also be mistaken for indifference. I knew one man who was so contemplative that he withdrew completely from his physical appearance to the extent that it no longer expressed anything. His body rested on me with all its weight; yes, it was active but impassive, as if he had abandoned it to me, and this absent face would park next to mine while I watched his ghost, transported by orgasm, floating above us like in a fantasy film. It was the same body that I saw when this man masturbated, indifferent to my presence and using a technique unique to him. He would lie on his stomach with his arms bent by his sides and squeeze his organ between his strong thighs by contracting them. It was a stocky body, and the muscles stood out all the more in this position. Being an expert in onanism, I admired the concentration he applied to the job, stubbornly and defiantly defending the mental isolation it requires.

When you have made love with a man a few times, you recognize when he is going to come, even if he is not one of those who announce it out loud. Perhaps you know before he does, informed by tiny signs: perhaps because he has slipped you into a position that acts like a trigger on him; perhaps because he falls silent, his breathing becomes audible, appeased a few moments in advance. One friend who was an imaginative, talkative and active fucker, who would keep you there for an hour with his extraordinary erotic fabulations and would make you try out the most acrobatic positions and the most improbable substitutes (cucumbers, sausages, Perrier bottles, luminous white billy clubs, etc.), would suddenly grow quiet a few moments before orgasm. Whatever position I was in, he would bring me back underneath him, tunnel into me without forcing his way, and replace words with discreet moans. I was convinced that this final phase followed a decision taken with full knowledge of the facts, and I wouldn't have been surprised to have heard him say: "Right, that's enough fun and games, let's get down to business." After he had ejaculated, he would stay on top of me, unleashing a little "Hee, hee, hee" in my ear, which sounded like a forced laugh, but was more likely his way of gently returning us to the real world. It was the laugh of someone who laughs first, in the hopes of finding your complicity and your forgiveness for having dragged you on some unexpected escapade. And as if to help extract me from our dream, before he opened his eyes, he would scratch my scalp affectionately.

In the same way that I don't take exception to flirting with abjection, that it nourishes my fantasies, that I have never been put off from titillating the folds of an anus with my tongue ("Hmm! It smells of shit," I hear myself saying, "but it's good") and that I have willingly cast myself as a "bitch in heat," neither am I disgusted—far from it—if I can feast my eyes on a body that may be in some way damaged. Yes, I like it when the whole body in my arms is as firm as a well-polished dick, but yes, I am as happy to edge beneath the drooping gut of a man waiting on his back like a woman for me to suck him off. Yes, I value the abilities of a man who spreads the lips of the vulva with careful surgeon's fingers, and who takes the time to admire what he finds with a connoisseur's relish, before he rubs the clitoris with a precision that soon becomes unbearable. But the man who grabs your hips with about as much ceremony as if he were snatching hold of the rail on a listing boat is just as welcome, and the one who mounts you with the vacant distant expression of a mating animal! The one who lies virtually full-length on your back, gripping the fat of your buttocks so hard that you find bruises on them the next day, and who doesn't give a shit that you can keep your balance only thanks to the excruciating cramp in your thighs, which are supporting two bodies. After that you let yourself go, reduced to little more than a lump of flesh plonked onto the bed and turned over with no more response of its own than a ball of bread dough. Being the amorphous support of someone else's frenetic activity, forgetting that your own flesh can have a specific form, and watching your breasts spreading and flowing with the movement, rocked like the water in the bottom of a boat, or seeing the cellulite on your buttocks squeezed in a big pair of hands: at times like these, as my eyes float over the surface of my molten body, I have to catch the eye of this workman dazed by his obstinate laboring. That face does not do beatific ecstasy. It would frighten me if the denatured bird that I am did not fall in love with the scarecrow. One eye is half closed because of a tensing effect that affects only half the face—I have already seen this feature in people who have had strokes—and the corresponding corner of the mouth twists to expose the gums. If I am not afraid of this snarling grimace, that is because it doesn't express pain but rather a supreme effort, a prodigious tenacity, and I am proud to submit myself to this force.

Patient

For much of my life I fucked naïvely. What I mean by that was that sleeping with men was a natural activity that didn't bother me unduly. Obviously, from time to time I would come across some of the attendant psychological problems (lies, wounded pride, jealousy), but they could be written off as losses. I wasn't very sentimental. I needed affection and I found it, but without feeling any need to go and build love stories out of sexual relationships. When I did fall for someone, I think I was still conscious of succumbing to some charm, a physical seduction, even to the geometry of relations (for example, having affairs with a much older man and a younger man, and having fun shifting from playing the role of a little girl to that of a protector) without ever being fuly engaged. When I complained to a good friend how difficult it was managing four or five longer-term relationships at once, he would tell me that it wasn't the number of men that was difficult but finding a balance between them, and he would recommend that I take a sixth. So I just left everything up to chance. I paid no more attention to the quality of sexual relationships. In cases where the man didn't give me much pleasure, or even bothered me in some way, or when he made me do things that weren't really to my liking, that alone wasn't reason to call him into question. In most cases, it was the friendship in the relationship that was most important. It could obviously lead to a sexual relationship, and I even found that reassuring; I needed to sense that all of me was appreciated. Whether or not I found immediate sensory satisfaction was less important. That, too, was written off in profits and losses. I wouldn't be exaggerating if I said that until I was about thirty-five, I had not imagined that my own pleasure could be the aim of a sexual encounter. I had never understood that.

My hardly romantic attitude never stopped me from handing out "I love yous" to my heart's content, only at the precise moment when the little motor situated in my partner's groin revved up. Or I would keep saying his name out loud. I don't know what made me think that this would encourage him to pursue and achieve his pleasure. I was all the more prodigal with these purely opportune declarations of love because they remained on the surface, uttered neither under the effects of any emotion nor because I was carried away in my ecstasy. I clearheadedly applied what I believed to be a technical knack. As time goes by, we do away with this sort of artifice.

Romain was very gentle, almost indolent beneath a virile outward appearance, with his biker jacket slung over a bachelor's rumpled T-shirt, yet another who lived in a studio on Saint-Germain-des-Prés, the least cluttered one I knew. We fucked on a mattress on the carpet, in the middle of the room, as the overhead light hit me full in the face. The first time I just kept on looking at the lightbulb and didn't realize that he'd ejaculated. Weightless, his chest lay over mine, his head turned away. The only living thing that I could feel was the odd strand of his long hair brushing over my mouth and chin. I had hardly felt him penetrate, he had scarcely executed a few weak thrusts. I, too, lay motionless, embarrassed. I didn't want to disturb him if he hadn't finished, but if that was the case, wasn't it my job to make my presence known and get him going again? But if I started moving and he was all done, wasn't I going to look stupid? Eventually, I felt something running right at the top of my thigh, a bit of sperm spat out by my vagina.

Romain's cock was a good size, it got off quite happily but was completely passive. If I had wanted to personify his cock, I could have compared it to a novice who doesn't move from his chair when all the participants in a ceremony rise to their feet: you felt no more urge to rebuke him than you would the inept novice. As I spread my legs under this boy, I had almost a sense of comfort from feeling nothing, nothing nice, but nothing nasty, either.

In some situations, I can display a rare patience. I have in me sufficient resources to remain silent and give my mind a free rein, accepting the fact that others are living their lives alongside me. I can cope uncomplainingly with the manias, petty tyrannies or even outright attacks of others, and I can turn inwards when necessary. I let them get on with it, and do my thing. Looking back on it, I now realize just how patient I was in sexual relationships. Feeling nothing, not minding and accomplishing were the whole ritual to its conclusion. Not getting hung up about having the same tastes as my partner, getting on with it, etc. I was indifferent because mentally I was so well tucked away in my very core that I could control my body as a puppeteer does a puppet. So I went on seeing Romain. Thanks to the impression he gave of being a charming bastard, he had quite a lot of success with women, and I enjoyed imagining the surprise or the disappointment of those who thought they were taking on a real man. I saw the astonished eyes of one of these women, probing mine for the comfort afforded by sharing a disappointing experience: "But Romain . . . he doesn't move a muscle!" I listened to the devastated creature's confidences as placidly as a sage.

I have spoken of the boredom that sometimes gripped me when meeting up with friends, and of the escape route I discovered by going off with one of them for a fuck. But even fucking can be boring! Still, I prefer that particular boredom. I can take in stride a cunnilingus that turns me neither on nor off; decide against redirecting a finger that is toiling away not at my clitoris but just to the side, where it hurts a bit; and finally, I can be perfectly happy when my partner ejaculates even if I myself don't get much out of it because, in the long run, being not quite "there" gets tiresome; I can tolerate all that so long as either before or afterward the conversation is stimulating, my dinner companions are fascinating, or I can wander around in an apartment I really like, pretending to have a different life . . . My train of thought is so detached from contingencies that it won't be hampered by a mere body, even if that body is wrapped in the arms of another body. Better still, thought is all the freer if whomever you are talking to is concentrating on the body; surely it isn't then going to resent him for using it as an erotic accessory!

It is not necessarily womanizers who best satisfy women. It may even be that some of them—although not all—go

from one woman to the next only to experience the beginnings and to spare themselves the stage when some sort of
fulfillment is required. (No doubt you could say the same of
some man-eating women.) One of the first I met, an artist,
was also much older than I, and one of my friends had warned
me: "When men are a bit older, it's fantastic, they're so experienced that you don't have to do anything, just open up
your legs!" I had to make quite an effort not to contradict
her. In one of the rooms in his art studio, the one in which
he received visitors, there was a big table laden with things.
It was like a house of curiosities with a jumble of ornaments,
lamps, vases, exotic-shaped bottles and kitsch ashtrays, as well
as unusual tools and plans and sketches for his own work.
We often didn't bother to go as far as the bedroom; I would
go and mingle with this bric-a-brac. He would push me up
against the table. Was it because he was slightly shorter that
I can remember his half-closed eyelids so clearly, the bags
under his eyes like a reflection of his eyelids, and his childish,
begging expression? Our pelvises were more or less on a level,
and as soon as I felt the swelling under his trousers, I would
set my "little motor," as he called it, going. That is, I would
jerk my hips rhythmically as I always did. And he would respond to these movements so that we rubbed our pubic regions against each other. What ramblings did my mind go
off on once my excitement started to fade? Would I notice a
new picture pinned to the wall? Would I think about the
article I had to write? Or did I empty my mind and stare at
the excrescences of brown skin on the surface of his eyelids?
Did I think about the fact that we would have time to do
this again later and that then his organ would go so far as to

penetrate mine? He would threw his head back, push me a bit harder against the table, which dug into my buttocks, and let out a couple of whinnies. We could leave it at that.

And yet he was an attentive man, and while I took him and his friends as they came, he would examine me—as he examined everyone—with piercing scrutiny. I have never known a man to be less complimentary in the comments he made about your body, and these comments would be uttered without ulterior motive but with the exactitude of someone exercising his professional eye, and whatever flaws you might have would anyway not detract from the fact that you were a turn-on for him. On top of this, his visual acuity was coupled with great dexterity, from which I benefited when he touched me. But others—if I can put it like this—don't bother with the body you offer them if you have already rendered them a satisfactory service. Like, for example, the man who took me to an attic room on the avenue Paul-Doumer that served as his office. There he was pawing me—that wasn't what I came for, but I didn't mind. The normal procedure would see him taking me to the couch and lying me down on it. Well, no, he is the one who lies down on it, full-length on his back, swooning and, with what is always a rather pathetic gesture, holds out his prick without looking at it. So I take the latter in my mouth, and quite soon I hear him say: "Oh, I'm going to come! I know you don't mind, I'll fuck you later." As far as I am concerned, I can cope with this, but my mind is sufficiently alert to realize that he is behaving badly. He doesn't fuck me later.

I am docile not because I like submission—I have never tried to put myself in a masochistic situation—but out of an indifference to the uses we assign our bodies. Of course I never would have given myself to extreme practices such as inflicting or suffering pain, but apart from that, given the enormous scope of individual preferences—sexual eccentricities, even—I always had an open mind and was invariably up for it in mind and body. At the most I could have been reproached for a lack of motivation if someone's practices didn't find much resonance in my own fantasies. For a long time I saw a man who now and then felt the need to pee on me. I knew what to expect when he made me get out of bed to suck him off. When his cock was good and hard, he would take it out and hold it with one hand not far from me. I kept my mouth open. Kneeling there in front of him like that, I must have looked like someone about to take communion. There was always a brief pause during which he seemed to be mentally guiding the urine on its way. With this effort of concentration, he managed not to come. And the jet streamed onto me, full, firm and hot. Bitter. So bitter I have never tasted its equal, strong enough to make you retract your tongue all the way to the back of your throat. He manipulated his penis the way he would have a hose, and the flow was so abundant and lasted such a long time that I sometimes really had to duck and dive the way you would if someone were trying to spray you with water. Once when I lay down under the stream, he came and lay down on the floor with me when he had finished. Using both hands, he daubed me all over with his piss and covered me with kisses. I hate the feeling of wet hair on my neck, but there was nothing I could do to stop it trickling. I burst out laughing. This made him angry and brought his affections to an abrupt end. Years later he still held it against me! "There's one thing you're not good at, and that's being pissed on." I admit it. In my defense, I would like to make clear that I didn't laugh as a way, for example, of shrugging off my embarrassment (it wasn't the first time I had been drenched in that way!), even less to make fun of him or of us (every reasonably original sexual exploit, far from debasing me, was in fact a source of pride, like another milestone in my quest for the sexual grail). I laughed because, unable to draw any masochistic satisfaction from the situation, which I did not find humiliating, at least I did feel a sense of jubilation rolling in a disgusting liquid.

Some positions are less rewarding than others for someone who likes to play the big baby, hanging on to a good-size breast. The least you can say is that I am not a dominatrix, neither morally—I have never conned a man—nor sexually: in perverse little scenes, I never held the whip. And I was very uncomfortable when asked to spank people. The man I used to meet in the area around the Gare de l'Est wasn't satisfied just to lick at my furrow, he would lift his head from time to time and, pursing his lips, ask to be slapped. I don't remember the words he used; on the other hand, I do know that he would call me "my queen" for the occasion, which I found ridiculous. I would watch him stretching out his neck, and something about his face repelled me as his features softened while he waited, including his wet lips, which made him look like a drinker who gets a mustache downing his glass. That still didn't get me to hit him hard enough. I put a lot into it, but I was never able to satisfy this need. I would go at it with a back-and-forth motion, but the thought that I might scratch him with one of my rings held my hand back. On other occasions I would try with one hand and then the other, in the hopes of putting increasing force in each movement, but then it was difficult to stay balanced, with my buttocks as close as they could get to the edge of the bed or the chair, which meant that it wasn't easy for me to hit his head as it emerged from between my thighs. In the end, I just wasn't into it. Paradoxically, I am convinced that if he had pretended not to attach so much importance to it—if he had put a little humor into his request, or hammed it up so it became an act—I would have entered into the game more easily, would have let myself get into it and struck him harder.

Faced with my lack of aptitude, he let it go, and I don't know whether his masochism drove him to more demanding exploits with other women. For me, these slapping sequences merely added another delay in a relationship dictated by infrequent and unscheduled rendezvous. They would prolong, even if not for very long, my wait for his cock. As I have described, I would come to a rendezvous already in a state of exacerbated desire. From the very first full-on kisses, from the first moment when his arms crept up under my clothes, the pleasure was violent. Next, the unquenchable sucking rekindled my desire to an almost unbearable level. But when the moment of penetration finally came, my little internal thread had broken; I had waited too long. I probably should have looked at the cycle of my desire differently, considered his licking as a prelude, chosen to forgo copulation, accepted the intervals between two rendezvous as a delicious echo of his caresses and faced facts: the high point was that moment when, having opened the door to me, without saying hello or good-bye and while we were still muffled up in our coats, he would crush me roughly against him. In that case, the perfectionist that I am would not have seen the slaps as something that like a schoolgirl you learn but rather as something like the other preliminaries, smooches and simperings, that you just do.

If I have to play a dominant role, I prefer straddling a man lying on his back. The position has little bearing on the way partners behave in role-play. When I was very young and wanted to be clever, I used to call it the "Eiffel Tower position." A tower straddling the river Seine, the Seine a torrent churning the tower like a tide. The piston movement up and down, the woman's buttocks making a sharp noise every time they smack down on the man's thighs; the first convolutions of a belly dance, the calmest of movements adopted when you want to catch your breath or to prolong the fantasy; the tilting backward and forward, the fastest and—for me—most pleasurable movement . . . all this is almost as familiar to me as fellatio. In both cases, the woman controls the duration and the rhythm, which obviously gives her a double advantage: the dick reacts directly inside the cunt, and the woman's body is revealed at a favorable angle, seen from below by the man. And it is gratifying every now and again to hear someone saying: "It's you who's fucking me . . . you fuck so well!" You come and go on the shaft like a well-oiled machine. Because of this ease and control, if I close my eyes I can imagine that the shaft inside is disproportionately big and strong because it so utterly fills a cavity that itself seems to have expanded to the size of my entire torso, and which has been thoroughly emptied of air so that it is a perfect fit. It is also one of the positions in which a woman can best squeeze the thing by contracting the muscles in her vagina. These are like signals sent from afar, a way of letting your partner know— while you are unashamedly making prodigious use of something that belongs to him—that you are still thinking of him.

All of these maneuvers are impossible if a woman sitting astride a man with her cunt fully occupied then opens up her ass to let a second man penetrate her. Two friends who used to skewer me like this claimed that they could feel each other's dicks through my insides and that it was very exciting. I only ever half believed them. These relatively acrobatic positions, or positions like that one that limit your movements in your attempts to maintain them—or even immobilize you altogether—are more for show. You can amuse yourselves forming a group as models would have done at some academy in the past, and the pleasure is fueled more by the sight of these bodies, which fit as neatly as pieces of Lego, than the actual contact between them. Sandwiched like that, I couldn't see a great deal.

When I am busying myself on top, I am now careful not to lean my head too far forward. Even though my face is not too lined, I don't think it is as firm as it used to be, and if my partner's eyes were open, I wouldn't want to give him a view of my jowls. My other reservation about this position is that I can't maintain each movement for very long. In the up-and-down movement, the thighs work like levers and tire quickly, especially if they are astride a wide pair of hips. I can keep the tilting movement going for longer, but the problem there is that both the very localized sensation on the front of the stomach and the precise linkage to the male movement produce (by a sort of reverberation) an imperious need for gratification. So much so that I stop the motor, clasp onto the body lying beneath me and say: "Give it to me gently." Three or four little thrusts striking sharply in the depths of my cunt are all I need to feel much happier.

I admire men who can thrust in and out for a good long time without appearing to suffer. I always wonder how they manage to remain leaning on their arms like that, and to show such stamina moving their hips. And their knees, how do they manage with their knees? When I am in the dominant position that I have just described and the act is taking place on the floor, my knees start to hurt. It is the same during a long fellatio if I am kneeling in front of an upright man. In fact, it is when I go the distance and give a really long blow job that it's really hell. Sometimes I let go with one or both hands, for exactly the same reason as someone doing a balancing act would, to show how well the mouth can do the job on its own, or to swiftly accelerate the movement. Then my neck tenses and becomes painful. A stiffness, as when a dentist works slowly in your mouth, spreads to my jaw, and the stretched muscles in my cheeks and lips, especially if the size of the organ to which I am attending requires me to keep my mouth wide open. When I curl my lips inward, my teeth leave a swollen ridge along the mucous membrane on the inside of my lips. I like that particular injury. It is hot and tasty. When my mouth is free again, I run my tongue over it with the attention of an animal licking a wound. After exerting myself, I find myself again in this exquisite pain, which I deliberately heighten by pressing my tongue more firmly.

I endure all the risks of coitus in the same way, the eccentricities of each partner and the minor physical discomforts.

This can be put down to an ability to program the body independently of physical reactions. A body and the mind attached to it do not live in the same temporal sphere, and their reactions to the same external stimuli are not always synchronized. That is how we hear a shattering piece of news without batting an eyelid or, conversely, can carry on crying even after we have taken on board the fact that everything possible has been done to console us. If I set the assembly-line of pleasure in motion inside me, even if my body encounters some discomforts, they will not be enough to stop it. In other words, I will become aware of the discomfort only after the fact, after I seem to have reached the peak of pleasure, and in the aftermath you really don't care about the discomfort; you forget it before you have noticed it. How else could you explain the fact that for years the same men caused me the same problems and I never complained or tried to avoid them? I am someone who hates to feel wet anywhere other than under a shower, but I have frequently been splattered with great drops of sweat by one particular man. I have never seen anyone sweat as much as he did. I could distinguish the impact of each individual droplet as it fell onto me. He didn't seem to be bothered by feeling too hot, but I had an icy feeling all over my soaked chest. Perhaps I compensated for this discomfort by listening to the wet smacking of his thighs against mine; I have always been stimulated by noises. I could have asked him nicely to wipe himself from time to time, but I didn't. Nor did I ever get over the allergy I had to one particular cheek being rubbed against mine. Given that the problem was chronic, shouldn't I have smeared myself with cream in preparation for my rendezvous with the owner of the cheek, who made a point of shaving carefully? No, I always came away from his flat with half my face on fire. The marks took hours to fade. It could also be that, on the subject of the discontinuity between the mind and body, in this case, my feelings of guilt for visiting this man in secret could have added to the allergic reaction to make me go red. In those instances, the mind was catching up with the body in spite of itself.

Different Manifestations of Pleasure

It is all the easier to write about discomforts and displeasure because they seem to distend time, and time allows us to focus. Even if they do not register with us straightaway, they carve out a furrow within us that represents time. The slapping sessions never went on for long, and wallowing in sweat was by no means a key element of my relationship with that man, which doesn't alter the fact that while they were going on, I would be both active and passive, waiting (and watching). Talking about pleasure, extreme pleasure, is much more a work of art. Anyway, isn't it commonly compared to being transported outside oneself and the world and, therefore, outside time as well? And is there the added, aporetic problem of wanting to identify and recognize something that no one has yet described for you, or only sketchily?

I have mentioned the truly ravishing feeling of the first physical contact, and I have also evoked how I discovered a prolonged orgasm, thanks to a dildo; finally, I have tried as best I can to describe the mobilization at the aperture of my vagina that becomes as hard as a ring of metal when my excitement is at its peak. I came to these facts relatively late. For a large part of my life, I fucked without regard to pleasure. First I should concede that, for someone who has known so many partners, no outcome was ever as guaranteed as when I sought it alone. I control the pitch of my pleasure to the nearest fraction of a second, which isn't possible when you have to take into account someone else and when you depend on their moves, not your own. Here is my story. Let us say that I am a porn actress auditioning fifteen possible partners who offer themselves naked all in a row. In my fantasy I am the officer reviewing the troops, examining each in turn and squeezing his apparatus while I rub my clitoris with the end of my middle finger; it soon becomes sticky. I feel the way it dilates. Sometimes I think it just rises up, a pointed little growth like a seedling. In fact, the whole mons veneris and vulva swell under my palm, and I can abandon my circular movements for a few seconds to prod and feel the whole as I would a pear.

On with the story. I choose one, and I lead him by the cock to a sort of massage table where I lie down, my pussy on the edge. At that point (but this preamble will already have taken a long time, six or eight minutes, sometimes more), my level of excitement can be extremely high. It is very localized, like a weight pulling toward the depths of my vagina and seeming to close it like the aperture of a lens. And yet I know (but where does this knowledge come from? From spontaneously measuring the exact degree of excitement, which, bordering on exasperation, feels almost overcharged and can only stagnate? From the fact that it won't be in that position that gave me the impression of being filled to the brim by my imaginary partner?) that, if I carry on, I won't get to orgasm or, if I do, it won't be very intense. So I stop the movement abruptly and backtrack in my story. I lick a few stiffened dicks before choosing one. Back to the massage table. (There can be several flashbacks, each one slightly different.) This time there are two or three who will take it in turns in my cunt. I increase the pressure with my finger, my clitoris rolls over a firm base—a bone? I picture one of the boys hammering me. The friction becomes frenetic. I sometimes murmur a few basic words of encouragement, pronouncing the words quite clearly: "You're so good," "Go on . . ." When the time comes, my mind empties. Exit the fifteen stallions. I grimace with concentration, curl my mouth up in an ugly snarl; one of my legs becomes paralyzed, but in an unexpected switch, I sometimes spontaneously knead one of my breasts gently with my free hand. The orgasm comes as the result of a decision. If I can put it like this: I can see it coming. In fact, I do often have my eyes wide open, and they don't see the wall in front of me or the ceiling but a fantasy X-ray. If it has gone well, the pleasure comes from far away, from the very depths of that long gut with its ridged gray walls, right to the mouth, which opens and closes like the jaw of a fish. Every other muscle relaxes. There can be six or seven waves. Ideally, I stay there for a moment, sliding my fingers over my vulva, then I bring them up to my nose to revel in the sweetish smell. I don't wash my hands.

I masturbate with the punctuality of a civil servant. When I wake, or during the day, with my back up against a wall, my legs spread and slightly bent; never at night. I take just as much pleasure in doing it when I am penetrated in real life.

In those instances, it takes me longer to come; I find it more difficult to concentrate on my fantasy narrative because the organ lodged inside me does not exclude the one I imagine. The real one stands ready, motionless and patient until I give the signal, a "yeah" of total acquiescence or a toss of my head, and the spasms that I have provoked meet the charges of the penis's at their most powerful. Can I really be bringing together two such very different forms of pleasure? The one felt so distinctly that I can almost feel my internal space expanding in the same way that I would watch the tide rising over the beach; and the other, far more diffuse pleasure, as if my body were reverberating like a muted gong, like when we suffer extreme pain and the mind distances itself from it.

I have never identified the contractions of my vagina when making love. I have remained completely ignorant on that subject. Is it because I don't recognize that sort of orgasm in those circumstances? Is it because, filled by my partner's organ, my own does not have the same elasticity? Still, happily, I did eventually realize that it was one manifestation of the female orgasm. I was over thirty when a male friend and I had one of those intimate conversations that are very rare in life. He was worrying about how one could tell when a woman had come. "Is it when she has spasms? Is that the only proof?" he asked me. Hesitantly, but not wanting to look a fool, I said yes. I kept to myself the fact that I was thinking: "So that's what it is." Until then, when my body had emitted these sorts of signals, I had not identified them as such, even if it was while I was masturbating with the precision I have described. Having not knowingly striven for the thing they signified, I could not recognize them. Some caresses made me feel good, some positions were better than others, and that was it. I now understand that this laconic conversation (with a man—and this is not a coincidence—with whom I hadn't had a sexual relationship) must have sown in me the seed of an anxiety that took many long years to develop into the state of dissatisfaction I discussed at the end of the first chapter.

As I have also explained, for me masturbation was initially, and for a long time, not a question of addressing the clitoris directly, but of sliding the lips of the vulva against each other. It wasn't that I didn't know it existed, it was that I hadn't needed to worry about it in order to experience my pleasure. I belong to the generation of women targeted by feminist books with the aim of guiding them in the exploration of their own bodies. I have squatted on a mirror and looked at my genitals, but that only confused me. Perhaps I found it difficult to follow a very scientific description. Perhaps I was slightly prejudiced against the feminist approach, which I thought was intended for women who were inhibited or were experiencing difficulties in their sexual relationships; these didn't include me because, for me, fucking was easy. Maybe I didn't want to call this "easiness" into question: yes, I fucked for the pleasure of it, but didn't I also fuck so that fucking wasn't a problem? Perhaps on that occasion I closed my thighs the way you would close a medical dictionary: for fear of finding in yourself the illnesses they describe, which would deny you some very enjoyable habits . . .

I was absolutely right, because when I opened the dictionary of received wisdom much later, my worries started to well up. At that stage I had a relationship with one man, and then a second, and I got it into my head that I should feel the same spasms when I was making love to them as I did when I was masturbating. Was I sufficiently familiar with my own body to achieve this? And, as if my sexual life were happening in reverse, as if I had to ask myself the naïve questions after acquiring and then forgetting all my experience, I was full of doubt about my clitoral antenna. Did it respond when I aroused myself with a manic finger? For a while I thought I didn't have one, or that it had atrophied. A man who had the best intentions but nevertheless was not very adept, and whose finger kept missing the mark, didn't help. Eventually I got it: the clitoris was not an obvious landmark like a nail on a wall, a steeple in a landscape or a nose on a face; it was a sort of muddled knot with no true shape, a minute chaos where two little tongues of flesh meet like when a wave hits the backwash of a second.

Pleasure taken alone can be told, pleasure taken with another is elusive. Unlike when I bring about my own orgasm, when I am with someone else, I never say: "This is it." No defining moment, no fireworks. Rather a slow settling into a mellow state of pure sensation. The opposite of a local anesthetic that suppresses sensitivity but allows you to remain conscious: I am cut to the quick and my entire body becomes the rim of this laceration, while my mind is reduced to a sleepy stupor. I can move only on autopilot, but still able to utter a final social grace: "Does it matter if I don't move anymore?" Is that fulfillment? It is more like the state we reach shortly before passing out, when we feel as if the body is emptying itself? Invaded, yes, but by emptiness. I feel cold, like when the blood ebbs away. It flows downward. A valve has opened, and through it I am losing everything that made my body a compact mass. And I can hear the noise of this expulsion. Every time the member renews its advance within the soft pocket that I have become, the displaced air emits a clear sound. It is a while now since I gave up screaming, since I woke the neighbors' baby and they complained by banging on the wall. The friend I was with was annoyed and he called me a few days later to inform me that "I've spoken to a doctor friend about it; screaming like that is a sign of hysteria." I got over the habit without even noticing. Since then, other women's screams have often reminded of those cries—more deliberate than spontaneous—made by horseback riders to encourage their mounts as they hurtle past you on the track. All I give out now are farts. The first one catches me by surprise as I lie dazed with fulfillment, as if dreaming. Others follow. I am amazed at my largesse.

Would the doctor friend have qualified or corrected his diagnosis had he known that, for a while, when my partners abandoned me on the bed, the table or the floor after making love, they left a body that was as stiff as a corpse? Luckily, it wasn't like that every time, but as far as I can remember, when the pleasure had been intense, all of my muscles would lock up. I was never frightened. It didn't last long. The same symptoms occurred once when I had an abortion, and the gynecologist said that I was not getting enough calcium. It wasn't even painful. It just occurred, like proof that something incomprehensible had happened in my body, which no longer belonged to me. The paralysis prolonged my lethargy. I obviously wondered whether, in addition to the salt deficiency, there wasn't some subconscious motivation. Was I holding back my body before or after orgasm? To avoid it or to prolong it? The symptom disappeared, and I forgot to answer the question. Then the opposite sort of behavior occurred. Instead of tensing as I teetered on the edge of the abyss, I would break down in tears. I would let go of all my tension with noisy, uninhibited sobs. I cried in a way that adults hardly ever cry, the heart filled with sorrow. The tension had to be particularly high, exceptional, even; perhaps more so than other women, I have a long way to go to reach ecstasy, and my tears are a little like those of an exhausted athlete awarded her first medal. A few of my partners were terrified, afraid they had hurt me. But they were tears of hopeless joy. I had jettisoned everything, but everything was only this: the body I had offered was just a breath of air, and the one I held and kissed was already light-years away. So utterly desolate, how could I not express my distress?

Even the most violent onslaughts don't get the better of me. You have to absorb the shocks, and when I end up with the small of my back crushed down onto the mattress, I feel too weighty for any form of ascension. When I am well prepared, I prefer certain tiny adjustments that conversely imply I weigh nothing. A brief gesture from one particular man struck me as quite divine; he was much taller than I, and he would gently drum his fingers in the small of my back. His attentiveness was so well honed as to be mechanical: like a housewife doing her dusting. Three or four sharp taps and I rose into the air like a sheet of paper in a draft. It made my cunt take in another few millimeters of his cock. It was enough.

Viewing

I am of average height and I have a flexible body, you can catch hold of me and turn me every which way. What surprises me the most when I see myself on video is this malleability. I usually feel so ill at ease, so awkward (I have hardly danced since my adolescence, and I couldn't swim more than three strokes in the sea), that I don't recognize this inoffensive reptile stretching, retracting and reacting swiftly and completely to every demand. Lying on my side in an odalisque's pose, with my legs slightly bent to bring the curve of my buttocks into the foreground, my gaze turned in the same direction that this curve is offered, my hand open on my mouth as I wait to see what will happen. Then, still on my side but curled more tightly to offer a better grip, my waist twisted a quarter turn to the back, making my upper body stand out, and my neck turned so that I can at a glance check that the slit is visible. In that position, I can do little. The animal pretends to be an inanimate object. The man bends my legs a bit farther so that he can wedge one of his in the triangle they form; he looks as if he is gathering a parcel to make it easier to pick up. He keeps them bent with a firm hand and shakes the object in front of him violently so that it springs back against his belly. I like this state of inertia, even though when my pussy is penetrated from the side like this, it is not very receptive. It is the same when the man comes to lie down on his side, forming the bar of a T for which I, having turned back onto my back, form the downstroke, with one of my legs lying over his waist and the other over his thighs. Again I take on an animal identity, somewhere between a frog and those upside-down insects that beat the air with their short legs. As I have said, I do, however, prefer to be taken from the front. I feel each ram of the dick more clearly and can regain some understanding of what is going on. By lifting my head and, if need be, holding up my ankles or my calves, I can watch the action, framed between my widely splayed legs. I can take the initiative: arching my back, for example, to raise my hips, and moving them as much as possible. The relationship between the elements is reversed: it is no longer a stake driving into the earth, but the earth quaking to swallow it up. Then I lie flat again. Pulled onto my back like a deadweight, I become objectified once more. Later, on the video, I will see myself taking on the shape of an inverted vase. The base is my knees, which I have brought up to my face; my thighs are squeezed up to my trunk, forming a cone that gets wider as it reaches the buttocks and then narrows at the neck after flaring widely on each side—would that be the curve of the iliac bones?—leaving just enough room for the plunging rod.

The pleasure is only fleeting because the body so pummeled, prodded and manhandled is evanescent. The body that has reached orgasm has been as completely absorbed into its own deep, mysterious recesses as the body of a pianist is concentrated in the tips of his fingers. And do the pianist's fingers put any weight on the keys? At times it doesn't seem so. Watching a video in which I masturbate with an airy, floating hand, the man next to me says I look as if I am playing the guitar. My fingers are relaxed and they swing back and forth in the dark cloud like clockwork, their movements very precise. When I am not alone and I know that they will soon be replaced by a much bigger instrument, I never press too hard, I make the most of this sweetness. I never masturbate by inserting my fingers into my cunt, I make do with barely dipping in my middle finger in order to moisten the outside. If the movements become a bit more pronounced, the fine skin on the inside of the thighs ripples in waves. I see that I am gently touching my partner's organ in the same way.

As I get down to a blow job, I protect the bottom of his penis and his testicles in the crook of my hands in exactly the same way that I would pick up a lizard or a bird. One close-up shows me with my mouth full and my eyes wide open, looking at the screen; there is a degree of technical control in this gaze. In another, my eyes and mouth are closed, my mouth offered to the glans which explores it; I look as if I am sound asleep when I am actually concentrating hard to stay in focus. Later, wanting to take in the glans, I carefully open and push aside the labia, well aware of how fragile this object that I am about to wrap myself around is.

Another film shows the whole of my body, behaving as it never would dressed, as I carry out my normal day-to-day tastes. Jacques, the director, makes me go up and down the stairs of our building twenty times in a dress of transparent black linen (there aren't many people on the stairs at that time of day). As if I were wearing a normal, opaque dress and being followed by an X-ray camera, you can make out from behind the pneumatic animation of the buttocks, and in front, you can see the trembling in my breasts each time one of my feet comes down on a step, while my pubic hair disappears into a wide shadow when it rubs up against the cloth. Even though my flesh has density, the silhouette is transient. For the next sequence, Jacques asks me to stand in the little shelter where the concierge works during the day, first with the top of the dress rolled down to my waist and then without the dress, and he asks me to adopt the various poses of the job. Oh, if only you could leave home and go to work with nothing on like that! It wouldn't be just the weight of the clothes we would be freed from, it would also be the heaviness of the body, which they would take with them. I admit it: the role that Jacques makes me play coincides so precisely with my own fantasies that I am unusually disturbed, almost embarrassed to find myself more naked than my nakedness. We go back into the apartment. There, by contrast, my body stands out very clearly against the white sofa. In the middle the hand comes and goes slowly, weighed down by a huge ring, and it is only the intermittent glinting of this ring that compromises the clarity of the image. My thighs and legs are spread wide, inscribing an almost perfect square. That is what I see today, but at the time I knew that it was what the man behind the camera was seeing. When, without putting the camera down, he came to remove my hand, my passage in which he slid was tumescent as never before. The reason was immediately clear: I was already filled by the coincidence of my real body and these multiple, volatile images.